IMPORT
CAR
COLLECTOR'S
GUIDE

1992 EDITION

PUBLISHED BY: EDMUND PUBLICATIONS CORPORATION

200 Baker Avenue, Concord, MA 01742

Table of Contents

INTRODUCTION

The Import Car Collector's Guide is written to help you understand what to look for in an imported sports car before you purchase one. Our authors also help you avoid mistakes that might prove costly after your buy. Here are a few suggestions that apply universally, no matter what make of car or period of design interests you.

First, read all you can about your intended purchase before you start shopping. Subscribe to Hemmings Motor News, the bible of car collecting. This monthly consists exclusively of ads for cars, parts and services necessary for the collector. Write to them at Box 76, Bennington, VT 05201. Get the catalog from Classic Motorbooks, Box 1, Osceola, WI 54020.

Second, join a club dedicated to the marque of your interest. There's no better way to learn about the pleasures and pitfalls of collecting than to meet with other people who have been there before you, and who can give you the benefit of their experiences - both good and bad. Each chapter includes club information at its conclusion.

Third, don't be afraid to pay earnest money for pre-purchase advice from a professional if the car you desire carries a substantial price. As with antiques and the fine arts, there's always a few charlatans ready to pass off their junk at fairly high prices to the unwary buyer. Get a second opinion.

Fourth, recognize that car collecting is unlike collecting pewter or stamps that sit on the shelf and stare back at you, asking little in return. Your collector car can become a demanding mistress, and will probably become a larger part of your life than you anticipate. But, she'll also richly reward your investment of time and interest.

Fifth, expect and prepare to have fun in the collecting, restoring, maintaining and driving of your imported collector car. More than one of our enthusiast/authors reminds that the cars you read about in the following pages are meant to be driven for enjoyment, not just kept in the garage under a drape.

Happy Motoring!

Richard Lewis, Jr.
AAI

MARKET PRICES

About This Price Data

The price data in this book is supplied by Automobile Investment Services. These prices have been carefully researched, compiled and statistically analyzed. They are accurate as of the date of publication. However, neither the publisher nor Automobile Investment Services assumes any responsibility for errors of omission, commission or future changes in the marketplace.

Methodology

The price data contained in this book is the result of thousands of hours of research on all areas of the collector car marketplace — wholesale, retail, auctions, dealers, private parties, regional and national classifieds, clubs, shows, and other hobby sources. A wide range of sources is needed to get a clear picture of the entire market. All data collection and compilation is computer assisted. This allows us to draw upon a huge statistical base — assuring accurate values that you can rely on.

It is important to keep in mind that the values you see here represent market values — not just book values, appraised values, asking prices or auction results.

How To Use The Price Statistics

1.) Determine the exact make, year, model, and line. For example: 1968 Ferrari (year and make), 365 (make), GTC Coupe (line).
2.) Have the car inspected to determine what its relative condition is on a scale of 1 to 3 (1 = Best, 3 = Worst;
3.) Look up the year and make of the car in the following section of this book. The section is in alphabetical order by car make. Within each make, the listings are in year order, oldest first.
4.) Find the line in the listings for the car's exact model and line. The current market value of the basic car is listed in one of the columns under the Relative Condition, depending on the <u>actual</u> condition of this car. For example, if, upon inspection, the relative condition of the 1968 Ferrari 365 GTC Coupe is judged to be a 2, its base value is $195,000.

ALFA ROMEO

BY PAT BRADEN

HISTORY AND OVERVIEW

Alfa Romeo history dates back to 1910, and there are five world championships in the corporate trophy case. I mention this up front because history and image are about the best things the company has going for it right now. Recently purchased by Fiat, Alfa is still trying to escape the curse of being known as a badge-engineered Fiat. Alfa's is not an unknown fate; the same absorption into another company happened to Packard, Bentley and Jaguar, as well as to Fiat-owned stablemates Ferrari and Lancia. It is not likely that Alfa's end will be wholly ignominious; both Ferrari and Lancia have done quite well under Fiat. But Alfa has a glorious history and its absorption into another company is, in that context, a sad development.

In 1910, a group of Italian businessmen decided to pick up the pieces of a failed attempt by the French firm, Darracq, to build a taxicab in Italy. The new company was called the Lombardy Car Manufacturing Company, which works out to the acronym ALFA in Italian. The automobile industry in Italy was having a hard time trying to stay up with current technology, and the real center of the business was not Milan, but Turin, where Fiat had its shops. ALFA management decided that the company's mission would be to produce a thoroughly modern, sporty car, a mission that still drives the company today.

There is a great deal of interest in the heraldry of the company badge, which dates from 1910. It's worth giving its broad description here. Details of the badge have been eliminated over the years, but it has always been in two parts: a red cross and a serpent eating a child. Both motifs date back to the crusades and are associated with the city of Milan. The red cross is a direct Christian reference. The serpent motif memorializes a successful crusade: the child being devoured is an infidel Saracen. The devices that have been dropped over the years include two square knots and a wreath. The knots and the blue field behind the serpent signify royalty, while the wreath around older badges commemorates Alfa's 1925 world championship. The word Milano was dropped from the badge in the 1980s. Until very recently, there has been a hyphen between the words Alfa and Romeo on the badge, but the name is not hyphenated in regular use today.

Alfa retained Giuseppe Merosi as its engineer, and he designed a series of chassis with sturdy, four-cylinder engines, a ladder-type frame and enclosed driveshaft. The sporting appeal of these Alfas caught on and by the outbreak of the Great War the company was well established.

There is no need to dwell on these earliest cars because the only surviving examples are in the Alfa museum at Arese, outside of Milan. After the war, the company received an infusion of funds from a local businessman, Niccola Romeo, who added his name to the acronym, making the cars Alfa Romeos. I will mention the 1921 G1, a failed attempt to enter the Rolls-Royce luxury market, simply because one example of this model is still in private hands.

In 1923, Merosi designed the RL-series, a 3-1iter, 6-cylinder chassis which proved to be a potent competitor and an utterly reliable tourer. In the early 1960s, Englishman Peter Hull was using his RL-series car for daily transportation. The RL was so successful in competition that Alfa management decided to enter grand prix racing, which was then dominated by Fiat. Merosi's racer was a failure and a Fiat engineer, Vittorio Jano, was brought in to replace him. Jano's grand prix car, the P2, won the world championship in 1925.

In 1926, Jano created a new sports car using many of the design features of his world-championship car. The new 6-cylinder passenger-car engine was available in three states of tune, the most powerful with twin overhead camshafts, hemispheric combustion chambers and a supercharger. Though it displaced only 90 cubic inches, the 6C1500 (the designation indicates the number of cylinders and displacement in cubic centimeters) developed over 90 hp in supercharged form, and could hold over 90 mph all day long, an incredible feat for a 1920s vehicle. The basic engine was quickly enlarged to 100 cu. in. and began to rack up a virtually perfect record on the race track. In 1929, under the direction of Enzo Ferrari, the 6C1750 cars won every race they entered. Zagato-bodied examples of these cars have brought as much as $1 million, though $300,000 will buy a good example in the depressed market of 1991.

In 1933, Alfa introduced Jano's next design, an 8-cylinder car of 140 cu. in., the 8C2300. These cars were available only with supercharged engines and became the pattern on which the all-conquering Tipo B single-seat racer was based. The Tipo B, also known as the P3, was introduced in 1934. It carried two superchargers and a unique split rear driveshaft. Just behind the transmission a small differential directed power through two separate enclosed driveshafts to rear stub axles. The arrangement countered torque reaction under heavy acceleration to improve handling, though it is not clear that Alfa engineers fully understood the dynamics at the time.

During the era of the 8C2300 and Tipo B cars, Enzo Ferrari's Scuderia was the semi-official Alfa racing organization. Racing had led Alfa to the pinnacle of fame and success in the mid-1930s. Between 1925 and about 1935, Alfa Romeo was the premiere sporting marque world-wide. But when the Mercedes and Auto Union cars began to threaten this supremacy, Alfa entered a confused era, filled with alternate race-car designs, none of which proved very successful. Finally, Jano, like Merosi before him, was fired. The suddenly-obsolete Tipo B engine design was given over to a sport car called the 8C2900, certainly one of the most exotic passenger cars ever offered to the public. The 8C2900B is generally considered to be the progenitor of the post-war GT automobile.

These cars occasionally come on the market for those with something over $1 million to spend.

For all its racing success in the early 1930s, Alfa went through some very hard times and was finally taken into the government bureaucracy in 1933. To improve sales, a lower-priced Alfa was introduced in 1932 as a follow-on to the 6C1750. The 6C2300 was a cheapened passenger-car version of the 6C1750 and was only available unsupercharged with typically heavy closed bodies. In 1939, this model was improved to the 6C2500, which featured fully-independent suspension along with Alfa's typical twin-cam engine layout. The 6C2500 was a much more sporting proposition than the 6C2300, in part because of its independent rear suspension, and the model continued in production until 1952. It was the post-war 6C2500, with sleek bodies by Farina and Touring that inspired the chopped-and-shaved styling of the classic American hot-rod. There is a good supply of post-war 6C2500 cars and the diligent enthusiast with $100,000 or more can own a good one without too much searching.

Immediately after the war, Alfa regained its racing dominance, since the specter of German cars circulating a course was not awfully popular. In 1950 and 1951, Alfa won back-to-back world championships. The Alfa that accomplished this feat was a 90-cu. in. supercharged racer that was developed pre-war to run in the Voiturette class, a kind of Formula 2 of its day. In its 1951 tune, this diminutive Type 159 used two-stage supercharging to produce 404 hp at 11,000 rpm, returning a fuel economy of approximately three gallons per mile. Only one of these cars is in private hands, surely the most desirable of all Alfas and worth...but then, you shouldn't have to ask.

A flood of hope and enthusiasm washed over post-war Europe and companies jockeyed for positions of leadership. Alfa decided that it would survive only if it entered mass production. Up to this time, all Alfas were hand produced and virtually all were custom-bodied by the small specialist carrozeria that still dot the northern Italian automotive landscape.

Alfa's peoples' car appeared in 1950. It was revolutionary in that it was a unit-body sedan with a 4-cylinder cast-iron 115 cu. in. engine. With its 4-speed gearbox it could very nearly top 100 mph carrying four people. Not only was the car a rocket, but it was so utterly reliable that it became the standard taxi -- and police car -- for a generation of Italians. The model was the 1900, and it went through a minor refinement as the 1900C, which is the more powerful and desirable version. In spite of the fact that the 1900 sedan set production records for Alfa, very few are still around and interest focuses much more on the special-bodied coupes and convertibles built on this sturdy chassis. One of the most desirable is the 1900 Zagato coupe, though other treatments by Touring, Ghia, Farina and Castagna have their own following. These sporty coupes usually carry 5-speed gearboxes (four and five-speed column-mounted shifts were stock, but frequently converted) and are still practical tourers, though their increasing rarity argues against too-enthusiastic driving.

The 1900 was such a hit that Alfa felt compelled to offer an even more affordable car, which was introduced in 1954 as the Giulietta. The Giulietta is essentially a lightened and miniaturized 1900. It has a unit body, an all-alloy wet-sleeve engine and a solid rear axle. The car was originally offered with a 4-speed gearbox but when a larger engine was introduced in 1963 as the Giulia, a 5-speed became standard.

The Giulietta is where most Alfa enthusiasts came in. When it hit the American shores in 1957 it was more expensive than an MG, cheaper than a Jaguar, and ran somewhere between the two in performance. It was comfortable and reliable in an era when sport cars typically spent more time in the shop than on the road. Almost immediately, Alfa offered a hot-rodded version, the Veloce, which had fabulously large DCO Weber carburetors, and could very nearly stay up with a Jaguar on the back roads while casually devouring Corvettes on the twisties. Considering the fact that the Veloce engine wrested 100 hp from 70 cu. in., that was truly exceptional performance.

1959 Alfa Giuletta Spyder   *Pat Braden Photo*

Alfa collecting centers on the Giulietta right now, and restorable examples are still available. In early 1990, Road & Track predicted that the Veloce would bring $20,000 by the year 2000; only four months were required for the ads to begin appearing for $20,000 Veloces. The Giulietta spyder from Pininfarina is vice-free and a willing conspirator for a fast top-down tour to blow out the cobwebs of day-to-day living. The Bertone coupe was an affordable Grand Touring car with perhaps more comfort and certainly more reliability than similar coupes from Talbot Lago, Aston Martin, Jaguar, Ferrari and Maserati -- and all at a fraction of the cost. Special-bodied coupes appeared from Zagato and Bertone: the former was a serious race car, the latter, the Sprint Speciale, was a styling exercise that made a perfect long-distance tourer.

The Giulia added even more performance, especially torque. It also added more models than can possibly be mentioned in a short history. While the Giulietta sedan was somewhat nondescript, the boxy Giulia sedan is a cult car among Alfisti: if you own a Giulia Super (especially the TI Super race version) you are one of the Very

Wise. For all its brick-like styling, the Giulia Super has a Cd of 0.34. BMW and the Alfa 1900 notwithstanding, the Giulia Super was really the first modern sport sedan.

The Zagato-bodied Giulia, called the TZ, deserves mention because it is especially desirable. This is a car with a legitimate race history which is quite comfortable to drive on the street. It is striking, if not actually beautiful, and wonderfully fast. A very few even sleeker versions were made as the TZ2 model, but these were bare-bones race cars with dry-sump engines and twin-plug heads. About $250,000 for the TZ, $1 million for a TZ2.

A lightweight aluminum-paneled coupe, the GTA, looked almost exactly like the stock Bertone Giulia coupe, but was equipped with a twin-plug head, minimal interior trim and proved a most successful race car. When it began to use the larger 1750 engine, the model became the GTAm. Like the TZ, the GTA is streetable and competitive. It is one of the few cars that truly can be driven to the race, take the first-place cup, and get you back home in comfort.

The first Giulias looked exactly like Giuliettas, but the sedan and coupe were restyled in 1964, and the spyder turned into a pointed-tail Duetto in 1966. The Duetto tail was chopped off (Kamm-tail) in 1969, when all US Alfas received SPICA fuel injection and an enlarged 1750 engine. None of the styling was well received at the time, but the 1991 Alfa spyder is essentially still the same car it was in 1966. In 1972, the engine was enlarged again to 2 liters, which is how it will spend its final years.

For the period covered by the Giulietta and Giulia, Alfa also marketed a larger car, first with a 2-1iter cast iron engine and then an alloy 2.6 liter powerplant. The 2-1iter and 2600 coupes looked like the Giulia coupe, but were scaled up approximately 20%. The spyders were more angular, but retained enough styling cues from the smaller cars to be still easily identified as Alfas. In a short history such as this, it is easiest to describe the sedan versions of the cars as engagingly ugly.

By the 1970s, Alfa began to run into real financial difficulties, and the old 4-cylinder models were saved from oblivion by modern technology. Mechanical fuel injection was used from 1969 to 1982, and Bosch electronic fuel injection was adopted after that. Between 1970 and 1975, Alfa survived primarily on mystique, and not even the most rabid enthusiast can work up a lot of adrenalin over the cars of that era. The only exception is the 1974 GTV Coupe, the last year of that model.

1976 Alfa GTV Alfetta   *Pat Braden Photo*

In 1975, Alfa introduced a sedan and coupe with an entirely new deDion rear suspension, calling the model the Alfetta after the world-champion 1950-51 car. The Alfettas got off to an immediately bad start though they are certainly both exotic and engaging cars. The driveline, especially the rubber donuts in the driveshaft are trouble-prone, the shift mechanism is approximate, and the sedans suffer from heavy steering.

The Alfetta driveline received a V6 engine in 1981 in the new Milano, while the new V6 coupe looked just like the previous 4-cylinder GTV with the addition of a hood bulge, front air dam and almost unnoticeable trim changes. The GTV-6 was an obvious derivation of a recognized model, and thus an immediate hit, but the Milano was cursed with questionable styling and ergonomics, and was plagued with early reliability problems. The 3-1iter Milano engine reappeared in the 1991 164 sedan, arguably the only recognizable Alfa part in that car, Alfa having been purchased by Fiat in January, 1990.

In addition to the regular production models covered in this brief history, there is a whole other world of special-bodied Alfas, the works of Italian bodybuilders wrought for auto shows and wealthy customers. Over the years, all of the great bodybuilders have worked with Alfa chassis. A discussion of their efforts would fill a very large book (indeed, several books have been written just on the collaboration between Alfa and Zagato).

This history has ended on a somewhat negative note and the reader may be wondering why, after all, one would want to buy a recent Alfa. Certainly the mystique is a large part of the reason. From a historical perspective, modern Alfas do not fare well. The cars of Jano are a very hard act to follow, indeed. But, certainly the same can be said of Ferrari, Maserati and a host of other enthusiast cars which, to survive, have had to contend with safety and emissions regulations. Alfa still remains one of the sportiest cars you can drive on the streets. It has pace-setting styling and impeccable road manners.

MODELS MOST DESIRABLE
TO PURCHASE AND OWN

No matter what Alfa you own, at some time in the future it will increase in value and have a following of devotees who will bid up its price. Few marques can make such a sweeping statement with such confidence. If my premise that all Alfas are collectible is correct, then a simple re-reading of the above history will suffice to cover the most desirable cars to own. But, that wouldn't be very helpful. Clearly, there must be some Alfas which are more desirable than others, as well as some which are really not very desirable at all. I need to distinguish between the absolutely most desirable Alfas and those the average enthusiast is likely to be able to buy. I will include pre-war Alfas, because without cars from that era the Alfa story cannot be appreciated.

The cars listed below are so rare that their sale will be between moneyed enthusiasts and conducted with the same gravity as the purchase of large corporations. The values of these cars are very dependent on momentary market conditions and the willingness of the buyer and seller. No owner of any of the following cars would want to have its value fixed by someone else, least of all an impoverished writer.

Further, I think there is a real liability for someone to peg a car at, say $3.5 million when its owner values it at $6 million. For that reason, I'm going to withhold pricing the following cars, all of which are individually identifiable. Their prices range upwards from $1 million. You won't find these cars listed in the Sunday want-ads.

Tipo 159

One of these cars is in private hands. There is another 159 at the Alfa museum sharing pride of place with an earlier Type 158. The value of the Type 159 is in the Bugatti Royale range -- possibly beyond, which would qualify it as the most valuable car in private hands.

G1

Only one of these early 1920s cars exists, and it belongs to an Alfa enthusiast in Australia -- the oldest Alfa outside the factory museum. While its value is not as great as the Type 159, its rarity makes it indeed a most valuable car.

Bimotore

The Bimotore is an Alfa created in 1935 by Ferrari and owned by Englishman Austin Dobson. It uses two Tipo B engines, one in front of and the other behind the driver. A duplicate car in the Alfa museum is missing its rear engine (a wooden mockup takes its place), so the Dobson car is both unique and most desirable. The Bimotore is clearly more valuable than a Tipo B.

Tipo B

Nine of these cars showed up at the 1985 Monterey historic races. Three or four others were not there, so the total number of Tipo Bs in the world is not much more than a dozen. For the wealthy enthusiast, the Tipo B is an excellent car to own because it is quite reliable and great fun to drive.

8C2900 Spyder, Coupe

The 8C2900 series features fully-independent rear suspension, a transaxle and comfortable seating. A book has been written on these cars, The Immortal 2.9 (Simon Moore, published by Parkside Publications), and the enthusiast intent on owning what is undoubtedly the greatest "production" Alfa is advised to get a copy. They are demanding, if not outright intimidating to own, but certainly one of the greatest cars of any marque.

Bertone BAT

In the 1950s, Bertone built three bodies on Alfa 1900 chassis to test his aerodynamic theories. These three cars, the whereabouts of which are well known, are called BATs (roughly, for Bertone Aerodynamic Technology). The numbers of the cars -- BAT 5, BATY7, and BAT 9, suggest a much larger series than ever existed. All three cars have large tail fins, those on BAT 9 being the smallest.

RLSS

These cars are antique in design though certainly sporting. The Targa Florio (RLTF) model with a 7-main bearing crank is a serious race car.

TZ2

All TZ2s were Autodelta factory racers, some converted from the more-popular Giulia Tubolare Zagato (TZ). There were two special-bodied TZ2s: one by Bertone, called the Canguro, is currently under restoration in Germany; the other, by Pininfarina, is in the Matsuda museum in Japan.

Now, we can move on to the cars the diligent enthusiast can reasonably hope to buy.

8C2300

Only 188 of these supercharged straight-eights were made. The most desirable cars carry 2-seater Zagato bodywork on short chassis (2.75 meters), though 4-place longwheelbase chassis (3.1 meters) are common. To check originality on these cars, the same 7-digit serial number should be found stamped on all major pieces, including the chassis, engine and transmission. The cars are reliable and fast, though they have problematic brake systems. They bring about $1 million.

8C2600 Monza
8C2300 Monza

These two Monza models are derivations of the 8C2300. The 8C2300 has a slightly higher state of tune with a magneto driven by a gear low down on the exhaust side of the crankcase. The larger-displacement Monza model, if its 2-digit serial number is preceded by "SF," is a genuine Scuderia Ferrari car with a displacement of 2556 cc (68x88 mm). A slotted "Monza" radiator shell should be carried by these cars, but it is important to note that the Monza-style shell is a popular addition to the 8C2300 generally; a slotted shell does not a Monza make. Genuine Monzas are worth between $1 and $2 million.

6C1750

The 1750s were available as sedans, coupes, convertibles (roll-up windows) and spyders (side-curtains). The most desirable 6C1750, the Gran Sport supercharged model with a Zagato body, is one of the great classic sport cars of all time. If one were to consider maintainability, then a very good case could be made for the 6C1750 as the most desirable Alfa of all. Ultimately practical, they bring between $200,000 and $1 million, a bargain considering the prices of some less-enjoyable models.

1900 CSS Zagato

This most-sporting version of the 1900 series is a cult car: you either hate its looks or love it. They currently sell for about $300,000. A large variety of other coupe bodies was available on the 1900 pan, many quite beautiful, but these bring lower prices than the Zagato.

Giulia Tubolare Zagato

As a combination of beauty and reliability the Tubolare Zagato (TZ) rivals the 6C1750 Gran Sport Zagato. These cars are popular and plentiful, and represent the most exotic (expensive) Alfa a novice should try. Be prepared to part with about $300,000.

Giulietta Zagato

Early in the Giulietta's production run, Zagato was asked to rebuild a wrecked Giulietta Sprint for racing. The prototype became so successful that Zagato started rebodying cars for individual clients. The first of the aluminum-bodied series resembles nothing so much as an over-inflated football. A later version, with a longer tail chopped off in the Kamm school of aerodynamics, was the aesthetic predecessor of the TZ (see above). More fragile than the Giulia, these jewel-like cars bring about $150,000.

6C2500

These production cars spanned the second World War, but the 1939 pre-war cars carry no premium. Though the 6C2500 had a very advanced chassis design with fully independent suspension and torsion bars, it was not very fast because of its weight. The 6C2500 was available in everything from a limousine to a competition coupe. The most popular models were the Touring coupes and 2-seat convertibles. The most desirable bring about $100,000.

GTA

If the GTA has a fault it is that it looks almost exactly like a stock 1967 GT Alfa. That is virtually its only similarity: the GTA is a no-holds-barred race car which dominated race tracks around the world for years. Both 1.3 liter and 1.6 liter versions are available at around $50,000. The larger displacement 1.7 and 2.0 liter cars are properly designated GTAm, and are more identifiable because of grotesque fender flares and slightly higher prices.

750 Sprint Veloce

Giuliettas built between 1956 and 1959 have serial numbers beginning 750. The earliest 750-series Sprint Veloce coupes were fitted with dual Weber side-draft carburetors, aluminum body panels and sliding windows. These cars are both rare and desirable and bring about $50,000. Later Sprint Veloces with all-steel bodies and rollup windows are less desirable and bring about half that price.

Sprint Speciale

This unique Bertone body took its styling cues from the BATs (see above). The SS was available with both Giulietta and Giulia engines. Superbly aerodynamic but not very light, the SS is the ultimate long-distance tourer, capable of holding 90 mph all day long. The cars range in price from $20,000 to $30,000.

750 Spyder Veloce

The 750 Spyder Veloce was equipped with the same Weber-carbureted engine as the 750 Sprint Veloce, but was available in much larger numbers: 2907 were produced. These early Giulietta Veloces are not for everybody. They were textbooks in the difference between horsepower and torque: plenty of the former, none of the latter.

Pulling away from a stop was accomplished only by dropping the clutch with the engine turning at least 3500 rpm. On the other hand, these cars would seem to run all day at 7000 rpm. The first regular production Alfa to touch $20,000 in the bull market of 1988-89, they have leveled off in 1991 to just below that figure.

Giulia Spyder Veloce

The Giulia Spyder Veloce, with dual Weber carburetors and hot cams, was the fastest production Alfa ever, at 180 km/h surpassing even the 8C2900B by 5 km/h. This is a car without vices, filled with virtues. They bring between $15,000 and $20,000.

1971 Alfa Montreal   *Pat Braden Photo*

Montreal

A hit of the 1967 World's Fair in Montreal, this car debuted in 1971 with a fuel-injected V8 engine of 2.5 liters. Heavy steering and high maintenance costs make this strictly a long-distance tourer with no racing pretensions. Once overpriced in the high 30s, Montreals bring about $20,000 in 1991. The chart at the end of this outline has values for other, more readily available models.

MODELS MOST LIKELY TO OUTPERFORM THE MARKET

I'm sure that when this book was conceived, we were enjoying a bull market in collectible cars. So much for the best laid plans. The market has gone into hibernation and the 6C1750, for example, was selling at $1 million three or four years ago but now can't find buyers at $300,000. Thus, I need to preface this section with a brief indication of Alfas which have already significantly outperformed the 1991 market. All of the cars listed below have seen much higher asking prices between 1988 and 1990:

- 6C1750
- 8C2300
- 1900CSS Zagato
- TZ
- 2600 SZ and spyder
- Sprint Speciale
- Giulietta Veloce spyder and coupe
- 1974 GTV

If I may recite conventional wisdom, the cars most likely to outperform the 1991 market are well-restored specialty cars with a documented history, such as early Veloces and cars with Zagato bodies. I have a few dark horses to recommend, however, if you're bored with trading in grains or pork bellies.

Type 33 Stradale

This nominally road-going car is based on the Type 33 sport-racer of the mid-1960s, and had such low production that it has virtually escaped the speculators. If you can find one, any price under $250,000 will be cheap.

SPECIAL-BODIED ONE-OFFS AND SHOW CARS

Special-bodied Alfas once populated the car shows. The Canguro has already been mentioned, but the Scarabeo and Delfino come to mind, along with several Zagato trial balloons. There is no market value for these cars because, like the Stradale, they are so rare. A complete, unrestored but documented Alfa show car should be worth $100,000 even in 1991.

SZ (ES30)

This is an almost-current limited-production car available only in Europe. Selling price was about $80,000, and I can't think of a more sound investment providing you're willing to keep it outside the US. I know of one investor with two.

6C2300

This car had the unfortunate fate to be sandwiched between two of the greatest Alfas ever, the 6C1750 and the 8C2300. It has 6 cylinders like the 1750 and the displacement of the 8C, but the panache of neither. At some point, when the 6C and 8C showstoppers are priced out of sight, someone is going to discover this Cinderella, the only pre-war Alfa not to have caught the speculators' attention.

1900 TI

Using the same logic as the 6C2300, the 1900 TI is likely to be a wise investment. These cars were high-production, durable and very fast. More importantly, they have great historical significance.

Not many are advertised, but if I had one, I'd expect it to be worth around $20,000. At that price, it's a very attractive opportunity if you're willing to wait for five to ten years.

Assorted Alfas   *Pat Braden Photo*

Montreal

The Montreal has already proved its worth. Why, only a few years ago it was going for almost twice what you can buy one for today. I consider them to be underpriced at $20,000 and would expect them to double in value within three to five years.

Giulia GTC

This is a 2+2 convertible conversion of the GT Veloce coupe. The cars have one drawback: the conversion created a truly inferior chassis which has little torsional strength and is prone to rust. Just be sure you get a good one that's been de-rusted at about $12,000.

Giulia Spyder Veloce

The Giulietta Veloce touched $20,000 first, but the Giulia version is a much better car for only a few thousand dollars more. At some point, the essential virtue of this car is going to make it worth significantly more than the Giulietta. You may have a 10-year wait, but the outcome is certain.

Callaway Twin-Turbo V6

Some of the GTV-6s were heated up by Callaway with turbochargers. The cars are absolute rockets, and well-controlled rockets at that, thanks to Alfa's conservative suspension engineering. Turbos raise significant reliability questions, which are especially significant given the GTV-6's propensity to chew up the rubber donuts in its driveline. But, I'm compelled to think that 10 years down the road, a Callaway V-6 turbo will be very desirable.

Giulia Super

The Giulia is the sleeper Alfa model line: buy any Giulia you can find. More specifically, the Giulia Super sedan is quite likely to outperform the market simply because it is such a good car. It has everything -- performance, reliability, comfort --but good looks: the Giulia Super is a true ugly duckling. If you ever drive one, you'll never be without one. They're currently going for $5000 to $6000. Buy two.

1750 Coupe

Enthusiasts already recognize the fact that the 1750 was a more reliable car than the 2-1iter that replaced it, and actually more powerful. In the long run, quality will tell. Currently selling for around $7000 for average condition, the cars should outperform the market over a period of five years.

Alfetta Coupe

These cars are not exactly despised but they are derided. Everyone knows they have questionable styling, vague shifting, an affinity for rust and an unarguably expensive driveline. If you can get past all that conventional wisdom (and the undisputed appetite for driveline donuts) you'll find one of the most enjoyable Alfas ever. The deDion rear suspension is wonderfully comfortable, while the front torsion bar setup can be easily lowered to improve the car's appearance. The ergonomics on these cars is perhaps the best Alfa ever managed. You can find ratty examples for $1500, but $4000 should buy a prime 1979 example, which is the best year. Try to find one with the factory sliding sun-roof.

MODELS TO AVOID

If there are good ones, then there have to be less-than-good ones. That's logic, and it applies irrefutably to Alfas. Take what follows in context: if this were written 30 years ago, I would have cautioned against RLSS Alfas because they wear out camshafts, against 8C2300s because of their treacherous brakes and against 8C2900s because virtually every one of them has a cracked monobloc. Time mellows more than people.

Giulietta Sedan

Underpowered, the Giulietta Sedan looks like a scaled-down 1900 sedan, but it has none of the larger car's virtues.

1975-6 Alfetta

This was the first year of the model (very few 1975's but enough to mention), and the cars were plagued with rust and reliability problems. Deserved or not, the '76 has a reputation strong enough to avoid for the time being.

Milano

It is still too early to pass judgement on this car. It is also far too early to consider it as an investment, for the value of Milanos is still falling. This criticism, then, is gratuitous: ugly, awkward and unreliable. In 10 years I'll be sorry I said it, but I'll savor the thoughts until then.

1750 and 2000 Sedan

Alfa had the sport-sedan category in the bag until these two models came along. There's nothing really wrong with either: I have a 2000 sedan with 130,000 miles on it and it's still going strong. The dullest Alfas ever.

1980-81 Spyders

These cars took the SPICA fuel injection system to the limit of its ability to control emissions. These are the least serviceable Alfas ever built and the poorest performers of modern times.

Spyder Quadrifoglio Hardtop

Seeing this car is like discovering your kid sister on a street corner at midnight in fishnet stockings and a halter top. Every cliche of modern styling has been loaded onto this car. The cars are mercifully rare -- because so few were sold new.

CARS THAT HAVE BEEN ENTHUSIAST-MODIFIED

I need to end this category categorically. Alfa is a sports car with impeccable credentials, but that fact doesn't deter a class of owners from believing they know how to tune the car better than the factory. Even though a sports car is supposed to be a statement of individualism, avoid Alfas that are not absolutely box-stock.

COLLECTIBLE DRIVERS

The cheapest Alfas are those 10-15 years old, which means the 1976-81 model years. Now, quite a few Alfas older than that are excellent everyday drivers. As a second car to a $40,000 BMW sedan, a $7000 Giulia Super may seem almost trivial. It's not the absolute value of the car but its irreplaceability which should deter its use as a daily commuter. For that reason, I recommend against driving an Alfa older than the 1972 2-liter series for regular transportation, especially in traffic, which exposes it to the possibility of a catastrophic accident.

Topping my list of collectible drivers is the 1979 Alfetta Coupe, or sedan if you need four doors. With air conditioning and a sliding factory sun-roof, these cars are comfortable and rewarding.

The GTV-6, though significantly more expensive, is a much more refined car than the 4-cylinder Alfetta Coupe. I especially like the 1982 model, the only year with a very tall overdrive 5th.

Alfa spyders are essentially unchanged from 1966 to the present, a span which rivals the Volkswagen and Model T Ford for longevity. Of these spyders, the 1969 1750 and 1974 2-liter are the best performers. Beginning in 1982, Bosch EFI was fitted, making these cars excellent future drivers as their cost comes down to your budget. Though they all look alike, there is limited parts interchangeabilty between spyder models.

PURCHASE PITFALLS TO AVOID

The most common purchase pitfall is to buy a car that is too new. Alfas reach their nadir in value at about 15 years: if you buy one newer than that you'll have a car that is still depreciating. If you buy one significantly older than that you may not be able to recoup your investment after a restoration.

Unless it has a documented, successful racing history, don't buy a modified Alfa. It's amazing how many enthusiasts think they can out-engineer the folks at the factory. Avoid an Alfa with electrical problems: the older cars were bad enough to begin with and the exotic wiring of the newer cars makes them undecipherable except to people who charge a healthy hourly rate.

In order of severity, Alfas are plagued by rust, blown head gaskets, weak second-gear synchronizers, fragile rubber driveline donuts and leaking rack and pinion power steering units. All Alfas suffer from rust, but the damage is frequently more cosmetic than structural. Alfas from the midwest and east will have more serious rust than California Alfas, but they will all have some rust. The newest Alfas, beginning with the Milano, are supposed to be rust-resistant. It is too soon to know. Rust repair is simply a matter of bodywork: it is all repairable.

Don't be concerned with the inevitable exterior oil leak at the head gasket: they all do that. Beginning with the 2-1iter, blown head gaskets became an Alfa characteristic. The failure typically doesn't cause a compression loss, but allows oil to mix with coolant, destroying the oil's lubricity. Look for a chocolate-malt like foam in the radiator or on the dipstick. The failure is potentially catastrophic, so avoid Alfas that show the telltale foam.

Weak second-gear synchronizers have been an Alfa trademark since the Giulietta. The only real solution short of regular synchronizer replacement is to learn to double clutch.

Alfetta models use three shock and angle-absorbing rubber donuts in the driveshaft. They fail. The donuts are somewhat expensive and should be considered a routine maintenance item every 50,000 miles or so. Similar donuts in earlier Alfas have proved indestructible.

The Milano power steering unit leaked. Most of the leaking units will have been repaired by this time.Awareness of this failure should be noted. Early Milanos were also plagued with blown head gaskets.

Alfa uses pointy-ended fuses that are designed to corrode in their holders. The Giulias exacerbated the problem by placing the fuse block in the engine compartment. The problem is solved by routine maintenance, but no one polishes the fuse block with a toothbrush, do they? If they are Alfa owners, they should. Up to the Alfetta, Alfas used a very antique method of wiring, and individual electrical component failures from frayed or disconnected wires were somewhat common. After 1975, Alfa cleaned up its electrical act.

WHERE TO GO FOR HELP

An important part of Alfa ownership is finding others similarly afflicted. As a group, Alfa owners are friendly, outgoing and helpful There is a national Alfa Romeo Owners Club, and anyone who thinks of buying an Alfa should be a member. The club maintains a network of technical help telephones and is a general clearing house for buying/selling/problem-solving. The club's monthly publication carries ads from Alfa suppliers and there are local chapters scattered across the US. Write to Alfa Romeo Owner's Club, 2468 Gum Tree Lane, Fallbrook, CA 92028.

The largest US source of new Alfa parts is Alfa Ricambi in Glendale, CA. Call 1-800-225-ALFA.

The largest source of used Alfa parts is Alfa Heaven in Aniwa, WI. Call 1-715-449-2141 .

The bibliography of Alfa titles runs over 40 books, not counting shop manuals: no matter what model you're interested in, it's probably well documented. The largest source of enthusiast books is Classic Motorbooks, 1-800-826-6600.

ABOUT THE AUTHOR

Pat Braden has been writing about Alfas since 1959 when he formed the vintage section of the Alfa club. He is the author of two Alfa books and several other books about Italian cars, including Ferrari and Abarth. Over the years, he has owned examples of most Alfas from 1929 to 1982, some 50 in all, with a current collection of about 20. He is an advertising copywriter with Saatchi & Saatchi.

YEAR	LINE	Relative Condition: Worse ↔ Better		
		❸	❷	❶
1954—1962	Giulietta 750/101 Spyder Roadster	10000	15000	18000
1954—1962	Giuletta 750/101 Sprint Coupe	8000	11500	14000
1960—1962	2000 Sprint Coupe	7000	11500	15500
1958—1961	2000 Spyder Roadster	13500	17000	25000
1962—1966	2600 Sprint Coupe	10000	14000	19000
1962—1965	2600 Spyder Roadster	16000	22000	29000
1962—1964	Giulia 101 Sprint Coupe	8000	12000	15000
1962—1965	Giulia 101 Spyder Roadster	10000	15000	18000
1963—1968	Giulia Sprint GT/GTV Coupe	5000	8000	10000
1966—1967	Duetto Roadster	6500	10000	13000
1967—1971	1750 GTV Coupe	4500	7500	10000
1967—1969	1750 Spyder Roadster	4800	8000	10500
1970—1971	1750 Spyder Roadster	4000	6500	8500
1971—1974	2000 GTV Coupe	4500	7500	10500
1971—1975	Montreal Coupe	20000	26000	32000

Austin -Healey

by Dick Lunney

History and Introduction
of the Austin-Healey Marque

The Austin-Healey marque cars were the culmination of the seventy-year automotive career of the late Donald Healey. Donald was born in 1898 in the town of Perranporth in Cornwall located on the southwestern tip of England. He was educated in aircraft engineering and entered World War I as an apprentice with the Sopwith Aviation Company and served as a Royal Flying Corps pilot from 1914-1918.

After the war, the lack of demand for aircraft engineers forced him to seek other career opportunities, and his interest in speed led him to the decision to open a motorcar garage in his hometown. Somehow, he convinced his father to finance this venture in spite of the town's having only one motorcar, which belonged to his father.

He began competitive motoring almost immediately by entering local reliability trials and hill climbs. His Perranporth-prepared cars won numerous gold medals, and in 1929 he won the Brighton Rally. That same year he began competing in foreign events. He finished seventh in the 1930 Monte Carlo Rally in a Triumph Seven, and won the 1930 Alpine Cup in a Triumph Invicta. His most notable win came in the 1931 Monte Carlo Rally, in which he prepared a new low chassis Invicta in his garage in Perranporth, and with Vic Horsman and fellow Cornishman Lewis Pearce won the rally outright.

In 1933, he was hired by the Riley Motorcar Company in Warwick in their experimental department. Warwick was the center of

English motorcar engineering and manufacturing, with over 50 firms producing motorcars. The following year he joined Triumph as Experimental Manager, and later became Technical Director. In these positions, he was instrumental in the design and development of the Gloria and Dolomite series of Triumph cars.

During World War Two, Donald ran the Triumph factory for the Ministry of Aircraft Production producing aircraft carburetors and controls. It was during this period that his dream of building his own motorcars began to form, and with his Warwick associates he began to plan a stylish, fast and affordable motorcar.

Using a Riley 2.4 liter engine and a chassis constructed out of war-surplus materials, a small band of friends built the first Healey Saloon and Roadster, the Elliot and the Westland. Although these cars had only modest commercial success, they were the basis of the Healey Silverstone which obtained success commercially and competitively, winning numerous road races and rallies. In all, 100 Silverstone models were built and they are the most prized of all early Healey motorcars by collectors around the world.

Austin-Healey Silverstone   *Wade Brown Photo*

Unfortunately, the success of the Healey Silverstone was not enough to insure the financial success of the fledgling Donald Healey Motor Company. In an attempt to improve his cars' performance, Donald struck a deal with the Nash Motor Company of the United States to build a new sports car. Nash needed a sports car to broaden their somewhat stodgy line of American family cars. The first Nash-Healey prototype used a Silverstone chassis and a Nash Ambassador six-cylinder, 3.8 liter engine and transmission. This new Nash-Healey prototype finished fourth overall in the 1950 Le Mans race, winning the Motor Trophy for the first British car. The Le Mans success led to the design of a new body built by Pininfarina of Turin, Italy from which 250 Nash-Healey motorcars were assembled in the Warwick garage.

The profits generated by the Nash collaboration allowed Donald and his staff to design and build a new inexpensive prototype car with sleek styling known as the Healey 100. This car was introduced at the famous Earls Court Auto Show in London in 1952, where Len Lord of the Austin Motor Company signed a deal with Donald to use Austin engines in the car, and thus the Austin-Healey was created. Lord also proposed that Austin assume the production of this promising new sports car.

The concept Donald had of this car was to fill the gap in the sports car market between the low cost, underpowered MG's and the much more expensive and very fast Jaguars. As with all Healey designed cars, the principal of building strong, reliable cars with readily available mechanical components was paramount. The secondary objective of achieving a top speed over 100 mph with a price below $3000 US dollars was established during a trip to North America to evaluate the US market in 1950.

MOST DESIRABLE MODELS TO PURCHASE, OWN, RESTORE AND DRIVE.

The Healey 100

The first Austin-Healey became known among collectors as the

100-4 (BN1 and BN2),owing to the Austin A90 four-cylinder, 2.6 liter engine, which propelled the car to speeds over 100 mph. The most notable design characteristics are the sweeping lines that are accentuated by the sculptured arrow carved into the door and front wing. Another feature was the clever method of folding the windscreen to form a "scuttle". The net effect of the overall design made the car look like it was speeding down the road even when the car was parked.

In all, 14,612 of these models were produced between 1953 and 1956. Production occurred in three phases with pre-production and special car assembly at the Donald Healey Motor Co. in Warwick, and the volume production of the BN1 and the BN2 models occurring at the Longbridge plant of the Austin Motor Company. The BN1 had a three-forward-speed gearbox with overdrive, and the BN2 had a four-forward-speed gearbox with overdrive.

Two special production runs were made of the 100 series with additional modifications added to enhance the performance of the car. The 100-M incorporated the "Le Mans kit" modifications, which included a high lift camshaft; higher compression; special valve springs, cups, and seats; two 1 3/4" SU carburetors with a cold air box; and a special advance-curve distributor. The body of the car remained unchanged except for the addition of a louvered bonnet and leather strap. This "Le Mans" modification kit was available only on the BN2 model as either a factory installed or dealer installed option. Approximately 2,000 cars received this option package with collectors favoring the factory over the dealer installation. Only 1200 factory-modified 100-M cars were produced according to factory records.

The "S" version of the 100 is the most cherished by collectors because only 55 of this model were built. Using standard frames and assemblies from the Austin factory located in Longbridge, the Donald Healey Motor Company in Warwick assembled these all-alloy cars with special engines specifically built for racing. These cars also had a distinctive oval grille rather than the triangular shaped grilles of previous Healeys.

The "S" model was designed to replicate the factory "works" Le Mans entries of 1955. Some of the first 10 "S" models produced were sold to Briggs Cunningham, the actor Jackie Cooper, and restaurateur Vincent Sardi. They were part of the famous Manhattan Chowder Racing Club and they raced these cars together at Sebring, Bridgehampton, Lime Rock, Watkins Glen and other race tracks along the east coast in 1956. Today only 38 "S" model Austin-Healeys are known to still exist.

Originally, the 100 was offered only in solid colors with Carmine Red being the most popular, followed by the famous "Healey Blue" and Old English White. Sometime in 1954, the factory began producing two-tone models that accentuated the sculptured line on the side. Other popular colors included Spruce Green and Black.

The Austin-Healey 100 was available with a whole list of possible options including wood-rimmed steering wheel, Lucas or Marchanl flamethrower driving lights, hardtops, radio, and chrome valve cover. Collectors should be aware that aftermarket accessories not available from the factory or dealers at the original time of sale can significantly reduce the value of the car in today's market.

Six-Cylinder Healeys

In 1956, it became apparent to Donald Healey that the A90 engine was no longer competitive as a sports car power plant. The first six-cylinder Austin-Healey was introduced in September 1956 with the model designation of BN4 or 100-6. It is commonly referred to as the first "Big Healey" which includes both the 100-6 and 3000 models. Production of the 100-6 model began at the Longbridge plant on the same line used to produce the discontinued 100-4 model.

1967 Austin-Healey "BJ8" 3000 MKIII   *Les Duggins Photo*

Many of the features that had been standard on the 100 became regular production options to hold down the base price and maximize the profitability through the end of production of the BJ8 MK III 3000 model. Some design changes incorporated into the six-cylinder models that differed from the 100 were the air inlet cut into the hood to accommodate the longer engine and an oval shaped grill similar to that used in the 100-S models. The grilles on the 100-6 and 3000 MK I models had horizontal grille bars while the later 3000 models returned to the vertical grille bars similar to those used on the 100-4.

Initial reactions to the new six-cylinder version of the Austin-Healey were mixed because the new car's performance was not significantly improved over the 100-4, due to the added weight of the larger engine. In 1957, revisions to the engine cylinder head and induction system raised the power of the six-cylinder engine from 102 bhp to 117 bhp, with a resulting increase in top speed of 8 mph. These changes occurred simultaneously with moving production of the car to the new Austin "Sports Car Plant" at Abingdon. Two versions of the 100-6 model were produced including the four seat tourer (BN4) and the two seat tourer (BN6) which was introduced after the engine modifications and the move to Abingdon.

Model type codes of Austin-Healeys are derived from BMC standards and followed on from the BN1 and BN2 100 models to the BN4 through BN6 and BN7 to BT7, BJ7, and finally BJ8. The letter "B" indicates an engine displacement in the range of 2000 to 2999 cc, while the "N", "T", or "J" refer to the various body styles as either the "Two-Seat Tourer", "Four-Seat Tourer", or the "Convertible". Left-hand drive versions have the letter "L" after the model code resulting in a BJ8L indicating a 3000 MK III Convertible with left hand drive. One deviation from this standard occurred with the first 100-6 model, which was given the code BN4 when, in fact, it should have been BT4.

In 1959 the six-cylinder engine was further modified by increasing the displacement from 2639 cc to 2912 cc and raising the compression ratio from 8.5:1 to 9.0:1. This new three-liter engine marked the introduction of the 3000 series of "Big Healeys".

Of the "Big Healey" models produced, the most desirable from a collector standpoint is the late model 3000 commonly referred to as the BJ8. Like all "Big Healeys," it uses the Austin A110 engine (the 100-6 used the A105 engine) providing 2912 cc and 148 bhp. This model offered the owner the most amenities of any Austin-Healey, including roll-up windows which replaced the plastic side screens of earlier models, wood-trimmed facia dash, fold-down rear seat back for luggage, and the culmination of the mechanical improvements of all earlier six-cylinder models. Production of the BJ8 totaled 17,704 with nearly 90 percent coming to North America.

1963 Austin-Healey 3000 Sebring   Kaye Kovacs Photo

The second most popular six-cylinder model for the collector is the early two-seat touring version of the 100-6 and 3000. These models incorporated many of the classic design features of the 100, including the smaller cockpit. Since the number of cars produced in these body styles (BN) was relatively small, it has added value to the collector. Recently, the BN7 (3000 MK II two-seater) has become highly desirable because of this model's use of three SU HS4 carburetors and small production run (5,450 units). The use of three carburetors versus two was done in an attempt to improve performance, but the added cost and difficulty of keeping three carburetors correctly adjusted by inexperienced owners made this production change short-lived.

Popular colors incorporated on "Big Healeys" include British racing green, "Colorado" red, "Healey blue", golden beige, and old English white. The interiors of all 100 and 3000 Austin-Healeys included leather-covered seats and full carpeting. Options included wood-rimmed steering wheels, wire wheels, overdrive, radio, heater, and hardtop.

Sprites

Donald Healey first conceived the Sprite in 1956 as a small, low-cost sports car fitting into the market niche vacated by the disappearance of the Austin Seven Nippy and Ulster models. Like most other Healey motorcars, this car used components from a variety of other British cars including a Morris Minor steering rack, Austin A35 front suspension, MG clutch and master cylinder, and Healey 100 seats with greatly cheapened trim (vinyl versus leather seats and rubber floor mats versus carpet). The original model (AN5) became known as the "Bugeye" or "Frogeye" because of its distinctive headlight positioning.

1959 Austin-Healey "Bugeye" Sprite   Bill Manginelli Photo

Upon its introduction in 1958, the Sprite was hailed by the media as a new generation of sports car with excellent handling, snappy response and distinctive styling. Power was provided by an Austin

"A" series four-cylinder engine equipped with two SU HS1 1 1/8" carburetors producing over 42 bhp at 5,000 rpm. The chassis was a basic monocoupe design with body panels welded to a pressed floor, and a frame unit that required very little special tooling and was utilized throughout the life of the Sprite/MG Midget. In 1961, production of the MK I Sprite or "Bugeye" was ended and the MK II or "Box" Sprite was introduced. In all, 48,999 MK I Sprites were built, making it the most successful Austin-Healey ever.

The most popular colors of early Sprites include cherry red, old English white, iris blue, leaf green, and Nevada beige (yellow). Options that can make a Sprite more desirable to a collector include those that were available from the dealers to upgrade the performance of the original car, such as disc brakes and wire wheel conversions, front anti-roll bar, and fiberglass hardtop. However, aftermarket accessories like a fiberglass bonnet and non-original gauges can significantly reduce the value of a Sprite. Although subsequent Sprite models enjoyed a longer production run that continued until 1968, the MK I was by far the most popular and continues to be the favorite of collectors.

HEALEYS THAT WILL OUT-PERFORM THE MARKET

The most sought-after Austin-Healey models are the 100-S and 100-M four-cylinder cars that have documented factory histories and are in better than average condition. Concours within the Austin-Healey community has taken on renewed emphasis with the advent of universally accepted concours judging standards. Top-level cars can now be awarded certification of their concours status, and a potential buyer should seek such an evaluation before paying a premium for an Austin-Healey.

Throughout the production of the Austin-Healey motorcars, Donald Healey believed that competitive racing was an excellent way to promote the marque and test new design concepts. This commitment to racing manifested itself in a very successful prototype program out of the Warwick garage with many famous drivers successfully competing in Austin-Healeys, including Stirling Moss, Briggs Cunningham, Carroll Shelby, Steve McQueen, Pedro Rodrigues, Innes Ireland, and Bruce McLaren. Not only were all of the 100-S models produced in Warwick, but all of the Sebring, Le Mans, and rally "works" race cars were prepared by the Donald Healey Motor Company staff.

These prototype cars are very rare, usually numbering less than ten during any given model year. At the end of each racing season, the cars were offered for sale to the team drivers, the crews, and finally to the various dealers or distributors. Many of these cars exist in private collections or museums, but a few are still raced on the vintage circuits in Europe, Australia and North America. Some of these rare Austin-Healeys still remain undiscovered and periodically the news of a special car being bought and restored is published. These cars when sold over the last few years typically bring as much as ten times the value of a typical "street" version. However, careful documentation of the racing history along with verification of engine numbers, etc. is critical to establishing the true value of a prototype Austin-Healey.

Few Sprites will out-perform the market because of the large number produced and the relatively low initial price of the cars. However, MK I Bugeye Sprites that have been carefully restored to original condition and have been judged in a concours competition will command a significantly higher price. Sprites that have a racing history, especially one that may include a famous driver or owner will command a premium. Probably the most notable Sprites would be the prototype coupes built in 1964-1967. These all-alloy-bodied cars had tubular frames and an aerodynamic shape that was quite unique to the marque.

To enhance the authenticity and value of any Austin-Healey or BMC car produced at either the Longbridge or Abingdon facilities, an owner can obtain a copy of the official factory record of their car including color and factory installed accessories for US $30 per vehicle. This information is maintained as a historical service by the British Motor Heritage Trust, Castle Road, Studley, Warwickshire B80 7A1, ENGLAND.

REASONS FOR AUSTIN-HEALEY POPULARITY

Many reasons can be listed for the surge in popularity of the Austin-Healey marque among collectors. Since these cars were popular among servicemen and college students in the '50s and '60s due to their affordability and sporty handling, the current generation of "midlife crisis" middle-agers can remember owning a Healey or knowing someone who did own one. The classic lines and the unique six-cylinder sound of the "Big Healeys" are both distinctive and endearing to their owners. The unique styling of the early Sprites, combined with their very low price, opened the realm of sports car fun to a whole new generation.

The somewhat amazing racing successes at Le Mans, Sebring and the European rally circuit, plus the numerous land speed records achieved by Austin-Healeys on the Bonneville Salt Flats, provided the marque with considerable publicity during the '50s and '60s. Austin-Healeys regularly out-performed and out-lasted much more powerful and more expensive racers from the likes of Aston Martin, Jaguar, Ferrari and Mercedes. For many, the Austin-Healey became a realistically attainable objective, whether the new owner wanted to race the car or simply use it for his or her basic transportation.

The use of reliable and usually indestructible Austin engines, plus the current availability of virtually every mechanical part, allows the novice collector or restorer to be confident he or she can fix the car no matter what the malady. Finally, the emergence of numerous marque clubs across the country provides a safety net of expertise, spare parts and activities that make owning an Austin-Healey more enjoyable for the owner who wants to enjoy restoring and driving his or her car. The largest of these marque clubs is the Austin-Healey Club of America with over 3000 members in 38 area clubs or regions. Membership information can be obtained by writing the club secretary as listed at the end of this article.

PURCHASING PITFALLS TO ANTICIPATE

All Austin-Healeys share some common problems of which the collector or potential restorer should be aware and anticipate. The most notable problem is rust! These cars, especially the 100 and MK I Sprites, were not properly painted or rust-protected on the interior panels (inner sills, boot, frames, etc.) so many of these cars have literally rusted from the inside out. In addition, neither of these models had a top that fitted snugly enough to prevent the seepage of moisture often causing the floor boards to rust.

On both the 100 and later six-cylinder big Healey models a common fatigue area is the doglegs that extend from the frame as a lower support to the front and rear wings (fenders). Rust or corrosion in this area can cause the car to sag, and is most noticeable in the fitting of the doors to the rear wing. Also, the shrouds were fabricated from aluminum and are prone to cracking, especially along the grill, bonnet, and boot corners. The shrouds are also susceptible to electrolytic corrosion along the edge flanges where the steel outer wing panels bolt together.

The Bugeye Sprite came equipped with ribbed rubber floor mats that relatively quickly either wore out or dried out and cracked. This mat material has never been re-manufactured and virtually all existing Sprites have replacement carpet mats.

All Austin-Healey motorcars were equipped with Lucas electrical wiring harnesses and fixtures. Original harnesses were cloth covered and prone to rot. Numerous jokes abound about the Lucas system, but one need only realize that the technology employed on these cars was distinctly pre-WWII to determine the real cause of the electrical problems. This primitive design gives the owner both the joy and frustration of often never knowing whether the car will start or whether all the lights will work. It has been said that the bond that holds the owners of British cars together is that we are all facing a common enemy....Lucas.

North American Austin-Healey Clubs

The Austin-Healey Club of America is the largest organization in the world serving Healey enthusiasts. This club has over 3000 members in 38 local regions and chapters. A monthly color magazine, CHATTER, and an annual membership directory are produced for the members. Membership information can be obtained by writing the National Secretary, 603 Euclid Ave., Arlington Heights, Illinois 60004.

The Pacific Centre Austin-Healey Club has over 1000 members located primarily west of the Rocky mountains. This club produces a color magazine 10 times a year. Membership information can be obtained by writing to 361 North San Antonio Road, Los Altos, California 94022.

Austin-Healey Club of Oregon
2930 Skyline Drive
Corvallis, Oregon 97330.

Cascade Austin-Healey Club
PO Box 39
Lynnwood, Washington 90046.

Austin-Healey Sports and Touring Club
765 Edgewater Avenue
Ridgefield, New Jersey 07657.

North American Parts Suppliers

Moss Motors Ltd,
PO Box MG
7200 Hollister Avenue
Goleta, California 93117
800-235-6954, FAX 968-6910

Victoria British Ltd,
Box 14991
Lenexa, Kansas 66215
800-255-0088, FAX 913-599-3299

Healey Surgeons
7211 Carroll Avenue
Takoma Park, Maryland 20912
301-270-8811, FAX 301-270-8812

Sports Cars Restored
705 Dimmeydale
Deerfield, Illinois 60015
708-945-1360, FAX 708-945-9671

Hemphills Healey Haven Ltd
4-B Winters Lane
Catonsville, Maryland 21228
301-788-2291, FAX 301-788-0530

Motorhead
3221 Wilson Blvd.
Arlington, Virginia 22201
703-527-3140

The Austin-Healey Store
8225 Remmet Avenue
Canoga Park, California 91304
818-996-5212, FAX 818-992-8573

Sports & Classics Inc.
512 Boston Post Road
Darien, Connecticut 06820
203-655-8731, FAX 203-656-1896

AUSTIN-HEALEY RESTORATION SPECIALISTS

Fourintune
W63 N147 Washington Avenue
Cedarburg, Wisconsin 53012
414-375-0876

M&M Restoration
3165 Campbell Drive
Fairfax, Virginia 22031
703-591-9601

Sports Car Specialties
1423 Audubon Pkwy
Louisville, Kentucky 40213
502-637-7516

Northern Illinois Austin-Healey Restorations
Elk Grove Village, Illinois
708-593-0630

Mini Motors Classic Coachworks
2775 Cherry Avenue
Salem, Oregon 97303
503-362-3187

Absolutely British
1720 S. Grove Avenue
Ontario, California 91761
714-947-0200

British Car Specialists
2060 N. Wilson Way
Stockton, California 95205
209-948-8767

ABOUT THE AUTHOR

Dick Lunney purchased his first Austin-Healey, a white bugeye Sprite with red interior, in 1964 while attending Kent State. During the summer, he refinished the car while working in a body shop in his home town of Syracuse. Eight years later, he was a grad student with a 3000, a wife and a new baby. Something had to go, and with regret he sold the 3000. Not until 1982 was he able to buy his "keeper," another bugeye Sprite, on which he finished a ground-up restoration in 1987, and which has been a winner in regional and national competitions. Dick Lunney serves as a concours judge and race promoter, and edits CHATTER, the monthly magazine of the Austin-Healey Club of America.

YEAR	LINE	Relative Condition: Worse ↔ Better		
		❸	❷	❶
1953—1956	100 Roadster	15000	19000	24500
1956—1959	100-6 Roadster	11500	15200	20000
1960—1967	3000 Mark I/II Roadster	12000	15000	21000
1964—1967	3000 Mark III Roadster	14500	18000	24000
1958—1961	Sprite Bugeye Roadster	5000	7700	10000
1961—1964	Sprite Mark II/1100 Roadster	2600	3800	5500
1964—1966	Sprite Mark III Roadster	2500	3800	5500
1967—1970	Sprite Mark IV Roadster	2600	4000	5500

BMW

BY BILL SIURU

THE ULTIMATE DRIVING MACHINE

We will shift gears a bit in discussing collectible Bimmers. They tend to be a bit newer. At any BMW concours show, truly vintage BMWs are rare, and most cars displayed would just be old used cars if they wore another logo. Rigid originality is not crucial to many BMW officiandos. They upgrade their cars with Recaro seats, updated suspensions, slick aerodynamic mods, mega-watt stereo systems, and so forth. These modifications don't really decrease the value of the car, if done well. Owners even expect to recoup most of their investment when they tire of their toys. Try that with a modified Mustang or Corvette. Finally, BMW owners believe in driving their cars, and do so with "gusto." Even pristine cars may have high odometer readings, and some have track time accumulated in driver's schools or autocrossing. After all, this is the "Ultimate Driving Machine."

HISTORY OF THE MARQUE

BMW's familiar "blau mit weiss" roundel, a highly stylized propeller, can be traced back to 1917 when the Bayerische Motoren Werke was founded to build aircraft engines. BMW's legendary motorcycles did not appear until 1923, and the first BMW car debuted in 1929. BMW's aircraft engines were as successful as its motorcycles and cars. They powered such aircraft as the Fokker D-VII biplane, one of Germany's best World War I fighters. Between the wars, BMW built the 9-cylinder, air-cooled Pratt & Whitney Hornet radial engine under license, even improving it so output was boosted from its original 450 horsepower to almost 1000 hp. Among its many uses was the tri-engined Junkers Ju 52/3m "Iron Annie", after the DC-3 the most popular civil airliner of the 1930s. Thousands of Ju 52/3ms were used by the Luftwaffe during the war.

The 14-cylinder BMW 801 radial engine was BMW's last

mass-produced piston aircraft engine and about 20,000 were built and installed in no less than a dozen different aircraft including the Focke Wulf Fw 190 fighter. BMW built the world's first mass-produced jet engine. Some 1300 BMW 003s were built for the ill-fated Heinkel He 162, better known as the "Volksjager" or "people's fighter", an ultra low-cost fighter built as a desperation weapon in the very last days of the war.

BMW's entry as an automaker started on a rather diminutive scale when it acquired Fahrzeugfabrik Eisenbach in 1928 and inherited the 15-horsepower Dixi, really the British Austin Seven "people's car" built under license. Eisenach was an old German automaker which produced cars under the Wartburg and Dixi labels for three-decades before it was absorbed by BMW. The "Ihle Dixi" based on the 1930-1931 Dixi 3/15 DA 2 was the first BMW to wear a kidney shaped grille.

BMW's most successful prewar car was the BMW 328 roadster, considered to be one of the world's all-time great sports cars. Its advanced features greatly influenced racing sports car designs of the immediate postwar era. This world class sports car combined spectacular performance, great reliability, impeccable handling, great looks, and innovative engineering in an affordable package. Only 459 BMW 328s were built between 1936 and 1940. However, the 328's features, especially its highly tuneable "sechzylinder" engine was used in a bevy of performance cars.

In the 1930s, Frazer Nash sold BMW cars under its own label, and thus postwar Frazer Nashes used the engine, plus many other pieces. The Frazer Nash-BMW connection evolved into the Bristol. The initial Bristol 400 was a warmed over BMW 327coupe. The next few Bristols, while getting redesigned bodies, still used the BMW engine until it was finally replaced by Chrysler hemi-head V-8s in the 1961 BMW 407. Before the AC was discovered by Carroll Shelby, the best performing AC Ace roadsters and Aceca coupes had a Bristol/BMW six under the hood. Modified 328-based engines were also used in British race cars like the Cooper-Bristol, Kieft-Bristol, Trojiero-Bristol, Lister-Bristol and Lotus Mark 10. In the US, "Wacky" Arnolt used the BMW, alias Bristol, engine in his

Arnolt-Bristol roadster.

BMW was one of the last major automakers to recover after World War II. That part of BMW that wasn't destroyed by Allied bombing, or taken as war booty, wound up behind the Iron Curtain. Various BMW prewar models were produced in Eisenach, DDR under the Eisenach label for several years before BMW in Munich was back in business. EMW even used the Roundel, only in red and white, until BMW took them to court and got their name changed to AWE. By the early 1950s, BMW was back to producing cars. The initial models were its 500-series of baroque sedans powered first by a version of the 328 engine, and then by Germany's first postwar V-8 engine. At the other end of the spectrum, BMW also produced the Isetta bubblecar.

BMW's to Collect

BMW 507

Many consider the 1956-1958 BMW 507 roadster to be the most beautiful BMW ever built. It was designed by Count Albrecht Goertz, who also penned the Datsun 240Z. The well-integrated lines are timeless. It looks great even with the top up, especially the optional removable steel top. The 507 used the BMW 3.2 liter, 150-hp aluminum V-8, reportedly patterned after the Oldsmobile "Rocket" V-8. All 507s were fitted with a four-speed transmission.

The 507 had a top speed at the magic 200 km/hr (124 mph) mark. The straight-line performance was outstanding, though handling on curvy roads was a bit cumbersome. But, remember this is a 1950s car. Perhaps the car's most serious flaw was its price. While aimed at arch rival Mercedes-Benz's 300SL, at $9,000, the 507 was $1,000 higher. Only 253 were built in 2 1/2 years of production, and it is rumored that BMW lost money on every one. This is a world-class exotic in the same league as the Mercedes-Benz 300SL or a contemporary Ferrari.

BMW Coupes

Through the years, BMW has offered many striking coupes that were usually based on the mechanics from BMW's more sedate sedans.

BMW 503

When BMW got back into the car business with the 501 and 502 "Baroque Angel" in 1952, the company was already thinking of a luxury coupe. Initially, a few coupes and cabriolets were produced by outside coachbuilders like Autenrieth and Bauer on the 502 mechanics. BMW's first "official" postwar luxury coupe was the 503 designed by Count Goertz. Only 412 of these 2+2 coupes and companion cabriolets were produced between 1956 and 1959. Initially, the 503, which was far from a sports car because of its size and bulk, even used the 501/502's column shifter and drum brakes all around. After 1957, the "second series" got a floor shift and disc brakes up front. Aluminum bodies did keep the weight down a bit to around 3,300 pounds. That was still a lot of heft, even for BMW's new 140 (DIN) horsepower, 3.2-liter V-8, though it nearly met the magic 200 km/hr mark.

1957 BMW 503   *Bill Siuru Photo*

BMW 3200 CS

This was the last BMW to use the V-8 being produced from 1962 through 1965. The 3200 CS's body was designed by Italy's Nuccio Bertone. Only 603 were produced, and while a topless version was produced in prototype form, it never went into production. The 3200CS was really a bridge between old and new. The old was the V-8 and chassis from the 503. The new was the styling, which would be used on a series of BMW coupes starting with the 2000 CS.

BMW 2000C/CS.

By 1965, BMW was making automotive headlines with its "New Series" of sports sedans powered by a very capable four-cylinder, 1990cc, SOHC engine. A companion, limited-edition coupe was designed around the new series mechanics. The 2000C/CS would be Munich's only luxury coupe with a four-cylinder engine and the first BMW to use coachwork from Karmann. The styling was definitely influenced by the previous 3200, though many feel that the twin kidney grille and headlamp treatment was a bit heavy-handed. The 2000C used a 100 (DIN) hp, single Solex carbureted engine, and the 2000 CS with twin carburetors produced 120 (DIN) horsepower. Being heavier than the contemporary sedan four-cylinder sedans, neither was a hot performer. BMW produced nearly 12,000 of these four-passenger coupes, with 75 percent being the somewhat more desirable 2000CS.

1968 BMW 2000CS   *BMW AG Photo*

BMW 2800CS

With the 2800CS in 1968, BMW corrected essentially all that was wrong with the 2000 C/CS. Greater potency came with the new 2.8 liter, 170 (DIN) hp six-cylinder engine and the front end was redesigned. Sales were over the 9,000 mark. Interestingly, while the 2800 sedans had four-wheel disc brakes, the 2800 CS had to live with rear drums because it still used the 2000 C/CS's rear suspension setup.

BMW 3.0 Series

In 1971, BMW replaced the 2.8 liter engine with the new 2985cc version of the smooth-running six that used dual Zenith carburetors. The 3.0CSi came equipped with Bosch D-Jetronic fuel injection. The CSi model was not officially imported into the US, but many were brought in as gray market cars. Cars fitted with the optional three-speed Borg-Warner automatic transmission were designated as the 3.0 CSA. Since the rear was a bit cramped, this was really a 2+2. The 3.0 CSs sold in the US were "loaded" with items like power windows, air conditioning, leather upholstery, and sunroof. BMW sold 11,063 3.0 CSs and 8,199 CSis.

1972 BMW 3.0 CSL   *Bill Siuru Photo*

The star of this 3-series of coupes is the race bred 3.0 CSL. The 3.0 coupe went on a diet, losing 450 pounds, with a lightweight steel body shell and aluminum doors, trunklid, and hood. Front bumper, power steering and windows, soundproofing and insulation were eliminated, and light Scheel racing seats, thinner windshield and fiberglass rear bumper were substituted. On "street" 3.0 CSLs, there was a "town package" that returned the soundproofing and power steering, plus a less bone-shattering suspension. 3.0 CSLs coming into US required thicker window glass and a real front bumper. One thousand CSLs were produced for racing homologation purposes, and it is estimated that about half of these were shipped to Britain.

In addition there, were 39 full-fledged 3.0 CSL race cars complete with their distinctive graphics and aerodynamics, including the high rear spoiler, front fenders, brakes and front air dam. Engine displacement on the racers was increased to 3153 cc and the engine produced 206 horsepower at a screaming 6600 rpm. However, tuners were able to eke out up to 1000 horsepower by using 24-valve heads and turbocharging. Even in "stock" form, the 3.0CSL was capable of 0-60 mph times of 7.5 seconds and speeds over the 140 mph mark.

BMW 6-Series Coupes

BMW introduced its completely redesigned 6-Series coupes in the spring of 1976. The 6-series coupe's styling cannot be faulted, and it probably inspired other designs including the current Ford Thunderbird and the Acura Legend coupes. Unlike the previous BMW luxury coupes that were true hardtops, the 6-Series coupes have a center roof pillar that functions as a built-in roll bar. The initial version was the 630 CS with a 3-liter SOHC engine using a single Solex four-barrel carburetor. There was also a fuel-injected 3.3 liter 633 CSi for the European market.

For 1977, the 176 horsepower, 3-liter engine with Bosch L-Jetronic fuel injection was used in the North American-marketed 630 CSi. In response to complaints that the 630 CSi was a bit underpowered, the 633 CSi was sold in the US after 1978. Meanwhile, the Europeans also had the 3.5 liter 635Ci and 2.8 liter 628Ci coupes to choose from. Americans officially got only the 633 CSi through 1984, though the better- performing European versions frequently came in as gray- market cars.

US buyers finally got a "federalized" 635 CSi in 1985. Only in 1987, there was the L6, the "L" for luxury, that came only with an automatic transmission. When the last 6-series coupe rolled down the Dingolfing assembly on April 18, 1989, a total of 76,417 6-series coupes had been built, making it by far the most popular BMW luxury coupe.

BMW 02 Cars

To many BMW fans, the last "real" Bimmer was the 2002, and one with round taillights at that! In 1966, the car-buff magazines were raving about BMW's new two-door 1600-2 sports sedans. The

1600-2 (later redesignated the 1602, the two standing for two doors) and the 2002 can be credited with starting BMW on the road from an off-brand marque to a household word in America. In 1962, BMW brought out its "New Series" of sedans starting with the 1500 followed by the succession of more potent four-door sedans that climaxed with the 1800 TISA built specifically for motorsports duty.

The 1600-2, spun off the New Series, redefined the term sports sedan, and maybe even the sports car. Even though it was a full four-seater, not a 2+2, three-box styling with a large trunk, it was equal to and often better than the contemporary sports cars in the "affordable" price range. Fit and finish as well well as reliability and durability were far superior.

For the 1600, BMW started with its new series four-door sedans. However, the 1600 was smaller in all dimensions, rode on a 2-inch shorter wheelbase and was 400-500 pounds lighter. There was four wheel independent rear suspension. The 1600-2 used a 1.6-liter four-cylinder engine that in base form with a single Solex carburetor produced 96 SAE horsepower at a high-revving 5800 rpm. Redline was 6000 rpm. The engine was coupled to a precise four-speed. Excellent braking with discs up front and drums in the rear completed the package.

Very shortly, the base 1602 was joined by the TI version that featured a higher compression engine with twin Solex carburetors that pumped out 118 horsepower. Meanwhile for the American market, BMW installed its 2-liter engine into the 1600 to regain the performance lost to ever more stringent US emission regulations to create the legendary 2002.

The end result was that the 2-liter engine produced 113 horsepower and the performance was on a par with the earlier 1600s, since the 2002 had also put on some weight. Again BMW brought out a ti (little letters now used) version of the 2002 that used a higher compression ratio and twin carburetors to produce 135 horsepower. However, Americans would have to wait until 1971 and the 2002tii for a higher performance version of the 2002.

The 2002tii used a Kugelfischer mechanical fuel injection system; that's the reason for the second "i". The bottom line was 147 horsepower, and that made it the most coveted car of the entire series. The 2002ti and the 2002tii also got a slightly increased wheel track, wider wheels, H-rated tires and bigger brakes.

In 1974, the series saw its most significant changes. US-bound cars got huge 5-mph bumpers that added almost 10 inches to the car's length and about 200 pounds more heft. At the rear, there were new (horrors) rectangular taillamps.

There are many models of the -02 series that were not imported officially, but sometimes appear in the used car ads since they were brought in as gray market cars or by returning servicemen. The Touring was a pioneering hatchback version which, while quite practical, had rather plain-Jane looks which makes it less collectible. The Tourings offered in 1600, 1800 and 2000/2002 form were not hot sellers.

Then there is the ultimate 2002, the 1973-1974 2002 Turbo. With the tii's Kugelfischer fuel injection and a KKK "kompressor", the turbo eked out 170 (DIN) horsepower. The Turbos also got extended fender flares, wide wheels, lowered suspension, front and rear spoilers and distinctive graphics. Only 1,672 of these 130 mph 2002s were produced with a few coming to our shores.

BMW Convertibles

Throughout its history BMW has offered open-top models, though usually in rather small numbers. As mentioned before, there were hand-built cabriolets built off the 501 and 502, and the 503 came in both hardtop and convertible form. And, of course, the 507 was a roadster.

BMW 1600 Cabriolet & 325 Convertible   *Bill Siuru Photo*

By 1967, Baur Karosserie was building a neat convertible version around the 1600-2 platform. With a facelift and an improved interior, it became the 1602 in 1971, and it lived on through 1975. A total of 1,682 BMW 1600/1602 cabriolets were built, but were not "officially" imported into the US.

By 1971, Baur was converting the 2002s into cabriolet form, in this case a very safe convertible complete with a Porsche-like Targa top. In reality, the BMW 2002 cabriolet was a sedan with the mid-section of the roof removable and a rear fabric section that could be folded down. The side windows and framing remained intact when the portions of the top were lowered.

Early versions even had fixed rear side windows, but later models used a wider, chrome tiara that eliminated the need for a second side window. In either case, the result was far from beautiful. Estimates are that about 4,200 were made with very few reaching the US. The Baur "safe" convertible concept continued with a 3-series version. For instance, BMW offered open-topped versions of the 316, 318i, 320, and 323i. Again, it was more sedan than convertible, and again, it was not the prettiest Bimmer.

In recent years, BMW has offered convertibles in the 3-series with both the six-cylinder 325i and four-cylinder 318 found in dealers' showrooms. European buyers can buy a BMW ragtop that is a guaranteed future collectible, the Z-1, or "Zed-One." This cutting-edge sports car features 17 plastic body panels over a high-tech monocoque chassis with a composite floorpan, aluminum driveshaft tunnel, reinforced tube instrument panel and a roll bar behind the top of the windshield. The Z-1's doors slide up and down into the high door sills. Unfortunately, the Z-1 is not sold in the US and recent changes in the laws have virtually eliminated any chance of finding gray market Z-1s that could be legally driven in the US.

M-Cars

In 1972, BMW established BMW Motorsport GmbH to support its factory racing teams and build limited edition high-performance versions of its regular cars for street use. These were the desirable "M" cars.

M1

The M1 is BMW's only midship-engined car and its only true exotic in the mold of cars from Ferrari and Lamborghini. Indeed, because BMW had limited experience with mid-engined cars, BMW turned to Lamborghini to engineer and build the car. However, when Lamborghini got into financial and labor difficulties in the late 1970s, BMW turned to Baur to assemble the M1. The car's multi-tube space-frame chassis was built by Marchesi in Italy and the fiberglass body came from Transfor-mazione Italiana Resini. Ital partially assembled the car before shipping it to Baur for final assembly. BMW Motorsports GmbH did the final testing and inspections.

M1 power came from a highly-modified 24-valve, twin-cam version of the stock BMW 3.5-liter six-cylinder engine installed longitudinally behind the cockpit. There was a ZF five-speed transmission, four-wheel independent suspension, oversized disc brakes and 16-inch diameter wheels with fat P7 tires. The bottom line was a fast (160 mph plus), excellent-handling, superb-braking supercar with the BMW fit, finish and reliability. Air conditioning, leather Recaro seats and full carpeting were standard.

Four-hundred M1 "street" cars were built for homologation purposes for production-class sports car competition. Unfortunately, BMW racing priorities changed, and the M1 never got to prove itself in serious competition. While the "stock" engine put out 277 horsepower, there was a Group 4 car whose engine was tuned to provide 470 horsepower with the bodywork, suspension and tires appropriately modified. Finally, there was the Group 5 racer that produced 850 horsepower from its turbocharged 3.2-liter engine. Only 450 M1s of all types were built between 1978 and 1981.

BMW M635CSi/M6

The M6 has rightfully been nicknamed the "Bavarian Ferrari." When originally introduced in 1983, it was designated the M635CSi. As might be guessed, the car was based on BMW's handsome 6-series coupe. Under the hood was a race bred M1 engine. The M635CSi was not "officially" available in the US until 1987, and by then the designation had been changed to the M6. Besides exotic class performance, the M6 also offered such ambiance as twin air conditioners, eight-way power front seats, eight-speaker sound system and a hand-stitched leather interior. As with all the "M" cars, luxurious accommodations and reliability are in no way sacrificed to performance and handling.

BMW M3 and M5

The M3 based on the 3-series two-door sedan and M5 that uses the four-door 5-series sedan are BMW Motorsport's "bread and butter" cars. While they are cars of the late 1980s and still in production, they are considered collectible because they are Bimmers.

Don't let air conditioning, power steering, ABS, electric sunroof, central locking, premium sound system, leather seats and power windows fool you. The M3 is a race-ready car right out of the box. It was originally built for homologation in FIA Group A competition. Under the hood is a 16-valve, 2.3-liter, dual overhead cam, four-cylinder engine that puts out 192 horsepower at 6750 rpm and is red-lined at 7000 rpm. European versions produce 215 horsepower.

The M3s use a manual Getrag five-speed, have a 25% limited-slip differential, modified suspension, brakes from the 6 and 7-series BMWs, and a beefed up drivetrain. Even though the M3 shares sheet metal with the 3-series, the body work is quite distinctive with its flared fenders, front air dam, rear spoiler, extra-wide door sills, front and rear windows that are bonded flush to the body and a greater rake on the rear window. Europeans can also order an M3 cabriolet or the M3 Sports Evolution with a higher performing engine and many chassis refinements, better brakes, manually adjustable three-position front and rear spoilers, larger wheel flares and better seats.

Someone should have told BMW Motorsport that exotic super cars don't have four doors. But since they didn't, BMW Motorsports went ahead and stuffed the M1's 32-valve 3.5-liter six-cylinder engine into the rather staid 5-series four-door sedan to create the M5, which first appeared in 1987. For Americans, the engine produced 256 horsepower, down about 30 horsepower from the European versions. Even so, the American M5 could turn in 0 to 60 mph times of around 6.5 seconds, and had a 150 mph top speed.

BMW early M5, late M5 (M1 rear)   BMW AG *Photo*

The Munich hot rod was also lowered a bit, its suspension tweaked and it was stripped of all chrome except for the kidney grill surrounds.   When BMW introduced its new and completely redesigned second-generation 5-series in 1989, BMW Motorsport started building M5s around this car as well.   The new M5 still uses the M1 engine, now with displacement increased about 80 cc and rated at 315 horsepower.

LESS EXPENSIVE COLLECTIBLES

If you don't have megabucks to own a 507, 6-series coupe or an M Car, there are other collectible Bimmers at lower prices.

The 1955 through 1962, BMW Isettas also wore the BMW Roundel. BMW bought the bubblecar's design from Italian refrigerator manufacturer Renzo Rivolta when Munich saw a market for an ultra low-cost transportation car in the post-war Germany. BMW added its own single-cylinder, air-cooled motorcycle engine, a 247 cc/12-hp in the initial Isetta 250, and a 297 cc/13-hp in the later Isetta 300. BMW sold almost 160,000 of these Isettas.

The BMW 600 was step a up from the minimal Isetta. It could carry four and had two doors - one in front like the Isetta and a side door. BMW even called it a "limousine." Power came from a two-cylinder air-cooled 582 cc 19.5-hp motorcycle engine, and nearly 35,000 went out the door. Perhaps the 600's greatest claim to fame was that it was the first to use BMW's famous Schraglenker-Hinterachse (semi-trailing-arm independent rear suspension) that is still in use in today's BMWs, albeit greatly refined through the years.

The tiny BMW 700 represents the transition between BMW "old" and BMW "new". For the old, the BMW 700 would be the last BMW car to use an air-cooled, motorcycle-type engine in the rear. In this case, it was the 600's "Boxermotor" that was enlarged to displace 697cc from its twin cylinders. The new was the 700's car-like styling done by Italian designer Giovanni Michelotti, and the 700 was the first BMW to use unitized construction. Much of the 700's underpinning came from the 600. The 700 had precision rack and pinion steering and decent brakes.

Most important, the 700 was the first post-war BMW to have a true sporting character, and it was the car that returned BMW to serious motorsport competition. The 700 virtually dominated its class and gave larger cars strong competition, its direct competitor being the contemporary Fiat-Abarth "Double-Bubbles".

The 700 had fine handling, and the engine could be tuned to produce as much as 78 horsepower with 2 spark plugs per cylinder, and 90 horsepower when the displacement was increased to 800 cc (the base engine was rated at 30-32 horsepower). The most desirable 700 models are the sport models that had a 40 horsepower engine obtained by using a 9:1 compression ratio, twin Solex carburetors, larger intake valves, and modifications to camshaft and pistons. Sport models also had close-ratio gearboxes, a rear anti-roll bar and tachometer red-lined at 7,200 rpm.

Body-wise, one of the 2,592 Baur cabriolet conversions of the sport version is probably the most coveted. The second choice is the neat-looking sport coupe or CS as it was called after 1964, with some 11,139 made. A rarer coupe was the longer wheelbase 700LS coupe, of which only 1730 were made. If you want an "exotic" BMW 700, how about one of the rare Martini-BMW 700 race-prepared coupes. Of the 188,121 700s made between 1959 and 1965, it is estimated that only about 3,600 found their way to the US.

INVESTMENTS YOU CAN DRIVE

All postwar BMWs are meant to be driven, though some more than others. While you might not use a valuable 507 or M1 for daily transport, they are quite reliable and fun to drive, especially, of course, the M1. Some of the early V-8 cars are a bit dated in the handling department, and replacement parts are hard to find because of their age and limited production numbers. The 1600/2002 are as much fun to drive today as when they were getting Miata-like reviews in the motoring press. Parts are abundant with lots of reproduction pieces being made.

Later model luxury coupes and M cars are great drivers with all the amenities of the newest cars. It is also sacrilegious not to drive these outstanding road cars. Cars like the Isettas, 600s and 700 may be too fragile, or slow, for everyday use.

BEST INVESTMENTS

What are the best bets as investments? The 2002s, especially the 2002tii, are perhaps underpriced considering their popularity with "real" BMW enthusiasts. Another BMW with great potential is the 6-series coupe. After looking at the new 850i coupe with its astronomical price tags and perhaps an overkill in technology, many people are looking at used 6-series coupes as a more practical alternative. Thus, these beauties should at least keep their values, if not rapidly appreciate. Indeed, as the prices of new Bimmers spiral upwards, many people will look at older models, especially when they can update them to contemporary performance and appearance standards without ruining their values.

What to look for in a collectible BMW? Since they are meant for driving, many are on the tired side. Like the cars themselves, repairs are often expensive. Designed for driving in the cool Black Forest rather than the Arizona desert, early BMW's suffered in the cooling department, often resulting in cracked and warped cylinder heads, for example. Rust is a problem on cars like the early coupes, especially those put together by Karmann, and the 1600/2002s, though replacement body parts for the latter are readily available and quite reasonably priced. Finally, there are many gray-market cars out there, so check to make sure all the paperwork is in order. Also watch for painted-over-rust cars that emigrated to America when they could not pass the tough German TUV inspection.

WHERE TO GO FOR HELP

Finally, there is tremendous club interest. and support. The BMW Car Club of America has about 27,000 members, making it one of the country's largest single-marque clubs. The interest is pretty much split between vintage Bimmers and newer Munich iron. The Roundel, the club's world-class magazine, has lots of ads for used Bimmers, most owned by enthusiasts. While many are priced on the high side, they usually have received lots of TLC, and are probably your best investment in the long run. For information on the club, contact:

BMW Car Club of America
345 Harvard Street
Cambridge, MA 02139
617-492-2500

ABOUT THE AUTHOR

Bill Siuru is a retired USAF Colonel who writes on aviation and automotive subjects. Growing up in Detroit, he got a Ph.D. in mechanical engineering, but was side-tracked into a 24-year career in Air Force R & D from his first love, which is automobiles, and writing about them. He has eight books and over 1,000 articles to his credit in such publications as: Autoweek, the BMW Roundel, Car Collector, Old Cars Weekly, etc. He has been a German car enthusiast since the 1970s. His first BMW was a 1977 530i, which he still has, and which is the standard against which he evaluates all other cars.

YEAR	LINE	Relative Condition: Worse ↔ Better		
		❸	❷	❶
1956—1959	507 Roadster	255000	290000	335000
1968—1971	2800 CS Coupe	8000	11500	15000
1967—1970	1600 Coupe	2800	4100	6000
1968—1973	2002 Coupe	2900	4200	6500
1974—1976	2002 Coupe	2700	3800	6200
1971—1974	2002 tii Coupe	4400	6000	8000
1971—1975	3.0 CS/CSI Coupe	8500	13500	18500
1971—1975	3.0 CSL Coupe	26000	33000	43000
1979—1982	M1 Coupe	130000	155000	175000

FERRARI

BY JOHN WEINBERGER

NOW AND THEN

The Ferrari F-40 was the last car to which Enzo Ferrari affixed his official imprimatur. This very special car marked the 40th anniversary of the Ferrari company, and the car will, in the years to come, become the ultimate collectible. The current price is over $400,000 and some have been sold to customers for as much as $1.5 million. This very unusual circumstance alone is a tribute to a great man with a racing appetite that will probably never be equalled.

Mr. Ferrari did not live to see the announcement of the 348, which is the current production model. For that reason, all of the cars prior to that time will have some extra sentimental value as well as real value. New models are being readied as you read this, but they will be introduced to the motoring world by his son Piero Lardi Ferrari. He has taken over as President of Ferrari and is also the managing director of the Ferrari Formula I racing effort. Even though Fiat owns almost 90% of the stock of the Ferrari company, Piero Lardi has retained, through his father's will, 10% interest. This enables the legacy to continue, and Piero's intense interest in the success of the racing team is obvious, assuring continuity into the next generation.

The next car that will be introduced to the world will be the 512 "America," which will replace the 412 2 + 2 model. This model has long been awaited by the US customer because it will be a car designed for North America. The V-12 powered 512 model is the first 12-cylinder-engined car for North America since the Daytona, which ceased production in 1973.

We all can be assured that more and more exciting cars will come from the Ferrari factory in the months and years to come. I am sure that the charisma will continue, because you can "feel it" when you talk with Piero Lardi. Though my visits have been brief, I feel that I am one of the few fortunate people in the world that have met both the founder and the son.

FERRARIS FOR COLLECTORS - A BRIEF HISTORY

It is especially interesting to know that the Ferrari market for collectors, and the acceleration in the value of virtually every Ferrari ever built, was predicted by almost all of the people that were closely connected with Ferrari from 1986 to 1990. The explosion in the value of these cars occurred upon the death of the founder, Enzo Ferrari, in September 1988. All knowledgeable people knew that the original Ferraris (the 12-cylinder cars) bearing his name were never manufactured in great quantity and would, therefore, become collector cars.

At the very peak of this explosion in the value of the Ferrari marque any old, rusty 12-cylinder car complete with engine, transmission and rear axle (the running gear) was worth $50,000 sight unseen! Since that time the market has quieted down considerably, and it is much easier to predict the future value of a Ferrari than it would have been in the beginning of 1990, or anytime in 1989.

Due to the lack of available cars, this so called "explosion" in the value of the 12-cylinder Ferrari carried over to the next best thing, which was a six-cylinder Ferrari called the "Dino". It was named after Enzo Ferrari's son Alfredino who was stricken with illness early in his life. Dino made considerable contributions to the design of the car. The 246 "Dino" (2.4-liter 6-cylinder) was beautiful, but never quite earned its fine reputation until the height of the recent peak in popularity of collector cars. The Dino came in two versions, GT and GTS. The GT was a fixed-head coupe. The "S" was a spyder version, which meant open top. The spyder, of course, was the most popular, and originally sold retail in 1973-1974 for $16,000 to $18,000. At the height of its peak early in 1990, this car was selling for $200,000.

1974 Ferrari 246 GT Dino spyder   Nicky Wright Photo

When the collector could no longer find a 12 or 6-cylinder car to restore (or to speculate with) for his collection, attention soon focused on the 8-cylinder cars that were made from 1975 onward. The first of these cars were called 308 Dino coupes and were built only as 2 + 2 models. It took nearly two years before the coupe and spyder models were introduced, leaving the buyer with little choice. The 2 + 2's, while very nice to drive, and in my opinion, one of the nicest driving all-around Ferraris, were never popular with the Ferrari enthusiast due to their 2 + 2 design by Bertone.

In 1976, Ferrari introduced the 308 GTB to the US market, and it was an immediate success. This Pininfarina Ferrari coupe was a classic design and in very short supply. At first, all of the cars were made with fiberglass bodies. In late 1976, steel bodies became available. The SE steel bodies were much more durable and heavier. The few fiberglass coupes that did come to the US are highly valued today.

The 308 spyder appeared in late 1977. Since the spyder's introduction, it has been close to 90% of the production, with only an occasional coupe. The 308 model was improved each year until the introduction of the 328 coupe and spyder, which essentially was a face-lifted 308 with a 3.2 litre engine. This model was produced until 1989, and was then replaced by an all new 348 model.

Obviously, the Ferrari V-12 has always been the car coveted most by collectors because of the sweet sound of the engine at speed, and due to the many racing successes that Ferrari had during the time that road-going 12-cylinder cars were built. These cars were all virtually coach-built with relatively few being made when compared to today's production of 4,000 new Ferraris per year.

It is important to know that Ferrari 12-cylinder cars were absent from the American market from 1975 to 1985 when the first boxer-engined 12-cylinder Testa Rossa was introduced. This new coupe was an immediate hit, and only the lucky few people who placed substantial deposits would be able to own one for the next six years. The cars were introduced at less than $100,000 and in six years the price rose to $187,500. In 1989-1990 this car traded for up to $300,000 for someone who wanted one and did not want to go on a "waiting list". This model is still currently being built and it is probably the best value on the Ferrari list today.

FERRARIS TO COLLECT

Now that we have established a little bit of chronology of the modern Ferrari (1975 onward), the first advice for the amateur collector of Ferrari cars is to establish a car's authenticity through several of the experts known to the Ferrari importer or the Ferrari dealers in the US. The older cars such as the 166, 212, 225, 250 and 275 models built prior to 1965 are so rare that no attempt will be made here to establish a value or future value. These cars should be approached only with expert knowledge or advice.

The remaining 12-cylinder Ferraris that could be considered "affordable" for first-time collectors with a limited budget are those that will be covered in an attempt to steer someone out of trouble while collecting, and perhaps assist one to own an interesting car to drive. In an attempt to simplify my selection as more or less desirable (for a collector), the following four categories are a beginner's guide for the potential collector.

RATING SYSTEM - MAXIMUM OF TEN STARS

1. Overall desired collectibility
2. Overall ownership experience
3. Ferrari desired collectibility
4. Ferrari ownership satisfaction

1965-1968   330 GT 2 + 2

1. ***** 2. ***** 3. **** 4. *****

The 330 GT 2 + 2 is a good example of a starter Ferrari that will make all of the V-12 noises that everyone loves about the marque. This car was always a lower-priced collectible, even though when it was new it cost nearly the same as a coupe (or two passenger version). At the peak of the popularity cycle, this car would bring as much as $150,000. Today, a very nice example can be purchased at $45,000-$55,000. The early cars are quickly identified by their mis-matched quad headlights (the later cars had more pleasing single headlights). The cars were coach-built by Pininfarina. When this car was driven every day, it was very satisfying.

1966-1968   330 GTC Coupe

1. ****** 2. ******* 3. ****** 4. *******

The 330 GTC coupe is, in the opinion of the many Ferrari enthusiasts, one of the most pleasing designs, and the most rewarding to drive as an all-around road Ferrari with plenty of room for a big man. It was offered with optional air conditioning and electric windows. While prices reached $350,000 for this model, it is now in the $125,000 range, and probably will settle in at this value unless something unforeseen happens in the market. The 330 spyder convertible is quite a different story. There were only 100 of these models built and as a result they are still commanding high prices close to $500,000.

365 model Ferraris were quite extensive and require more time and effort to study. The following 365 models were built from 1967 thru 1976.

1969 Ferrari 365 GTC   *Nicky Wright Photo*

1968-1970   365 GTC-GTS

1. ****** 2. ******* 3. ******* 4. *******

This car was virtually identical to the 330 GTC coupe, with larger displacement engine distinguished by two vents in the hood. Although only 150 of these models were built, condition is more important than engine size. A few (20) convertibles were produced and because of the small numbers, would bring a slight premium over the 330 convertible.

1967-1971   365 GT 2 + 2

1. *** 2. ***** 3. *** 4. ***

A very large car, good looking, but never very popular due to its 2 + 2 design. Most Ferrari 2 + 2 models have never attained collector or good resale status, but were very satisfying to drive as they were beautiful. Approximately 800 of these cars were made and can be purchased under $100,000. They probably will not appreciate in the foreseen future. One has to like this design personally to collect it for his only Ferrari car.

1971-1972   365 GTC/4

1. **** 2. ***** 3. **** 4. ******

One of the most forgotten Ferrari cars, the GTC/4, was nonetheless a great car. It came equipped with power steering and had a very lovely body. The engine compartment was most impressive, with side-draft Weber carburetors that seemed to fill up the enormous space provided for this massive 12-cylinder engine. This car did not reach the popularity heights enjoyed by its brethren, the Daytona coupe and spyder, but was a real true road-going Ferrari that reached values of $250,000-$300,000. Today, one could be purchased at somewhere in the $100,000 range at a very good value. Again, these cars must be inspected with an expert eye due to the costs of restoration both mechanically and cosmetically.

Most enthusiasts, as we said earlier, did not get excited about this car due to its almost 2 + 2 design. Only after all of the Daytona models reached their heights during the peak of trading did the GTC/4 become popular. It was in its own right a very pretty car, very comfortable to drive and it made all of the right noises. The price of the car was certainly a bargain compared to the Daytona and other earlier models.

1968-1973   365 GTB/4 Coupe Daytona

1. ********* 2. ********** 3. ********** 4. **********

This model was called the Daytona coupe and is one of the most popular Ferraris of aficionados and general enthusiasts. This fast-back model was sleek looking and very fast, with a great 12-cylinder sound from the exhaust. Most popular, of course, was the red exterior, black interior combination. The car was also stunning in fly yellow, and seemed to possess the lines for this color. This car was imported to the US and was distinguished by its headlight design which needed to conform to the new US standards for headlight height.

1971 Ferrari 365 GTS Daytona Convertible   *Nicky Wright Photo*

The European model, which some say was a more pleasing headlight design, is, however, not as valuable as the US version. These coupes originally sold in the $27,000 area when new, and during the recent peak sold as high at $600,000. These very desirable coupes can be purchased for $175,000 to $250,000 and would be considered first when any acceleration of the market would occur again. They are real Ferrari's in the true sense of the word. They are very fast, very comfortable, good looking. However, you need good strong arms to park one - it's a real man's Ferrari.

1972-1973   GTB/4 Spyder

1. ********** 2. ********** 3. ********** 4. **********

This very collectable car was built only for a short time and reportedly only 125 were made. There were, however, many coupes converted to spyder models, which is fairly easy to do, and they look quite good. One needs to be an expert to tell the difference between a "factory spyder" and a converted spyder. Generally, the converted spyder is worth the same as a coupe. The rationale is that the car is really no longer original, yet it is very desirable. As a result, there is no penalty for the conversion, nor is there any credit given to enhance its value. If one really desires a spyder model, this would be a great car to own and drive. The original "factory" spyder may be worth too much to drive without being nervous about someone stealing it, and it would be irreplaceable. The original spyder value today would be in the $750,000 area and a good value over time.

1972-1976   365 GT/4 2 + 2

1. ** 2. ** 3. ** 4. **

After the last GTC-4 was produced, it was replaced by this GT4 2 + 2. It was more a gentleman's Ferrari, and was available with automatic transmission, power steering and air conditioning, which made it a complete car for someone to drive everyday. The car was rather large and quite "muffled," and was popular in Europe but not exported to the US. Some cars were brought over and converted to US EPA and DOT specs. As an investment Ferrari it would not be of great value. If one needs to have a family Ferrari, this would be a good car at a reasonable price somewhere around $60,000. This car evolved into the 400 and 412 model.

1976-1984   400 Coupe (2 + 2)

1. ***   2. ***   3. ***   4.   ***

Essentially this was an updated 365 model with larger engine, also available in 5-speed or automatic. Only small changes were made in seat style and interior trim; otherwise it's the same as above. In 1980, the car was fitted with fuel injection and was much more flexible to drive and was also more reliable. Value would be almost the same as all 400 models depending more on condition.

1985-1989   412

1. ***** 2. ****** 3. **** 4. ****

This is a further update of the 400i serves with more interior changes. The seats were more comfortable, and the dash layout was very pleasing. The engine was also, slightly larger and now became the ultimate driving 2 + 2 with enough engine to make the automatic transmission respond quite well. This is a very desirable road car and although not quite a collector car, it will retain its value over the years because it is the final refinement of this series. At the present time, no 2 + 2 models are in production and rumor has it that a 512 model will appear in 1992 after an absence of three years.   Today the value of a nice 412 or 412A would be approximately $100,000.

It may be good to note at this point that the 365GT 2 + 2, 400, 400i and 412 models were never made for the US market. There were many cars sold, however, for "European Delivery," and subsequently shipped back to the states for conversion to the US specs. Most of this conversion work was done quite reputably by Dick Fritz of Amerispec Corp. in Danbury, Connecticut. When purchasing one of these cars (as well as any American version Ferrari manufactured after 1967), it is advised that the buyer obtain proper paperwork with the car that states it has passed thru US customs and released with proper EPA and DOT documentation. This advice includes models that might not be so apparently

European versions, such as Daytona, 308 and 328 models.

1974-1981   365 GT4/BB Berlinetta Boxer

1. ****** 2. **** 3. ***** 4. *****

As we stated before, 12-cylinder cars were not available in the US for ten years. When this "Boxer" model was introduced to Europe and other parts of the world, it whetted the appetite of the US buyer. As a result, the car created what we know as a "grey market" car. It was brought into the US and converted to US specs by small "cottage industry" companies around Texas, California and the East Coast.

These early boxers were very difficult to convert to US emission standards because the Weber carburetor design did not allow the engine to run "lean" enough to still run properly at idle and high speed. As a result, most of the cars never really ran very well in the "US converted" version. On rare occasions when one can be found to run right, it is very exciting, easy to drive, and an exceptionally fast sports car in all of the true senses of the word. The value of one of these today could be as much as $175,000.

1978 Ferrari 512BB Boxer   *Nicky Wright Photo*

1982-1984   BB 512i Berlinetta Boxer

1. ******** 2. ********** 3. ********** 4. **********

In 1982, Ferrari finally installed fuel injection on the Boxer, which made the car even more popular. It could now be tuned to run properly without many changes to meet EPA requirements. As a result, many of these cars were imported to the US and "converted". They were perfect! Not only did they look great, they also ran great. By 1983, there were quite a few "shops" converting these cars into legal US cars, and there was quite a healthy overseas delivery program. In the writers opinion, the "512 BBi" is really the car to own, collect or drive. It has very light steering, good air conditioning, handles very well, has great looks and reliability.

This car is more satisfying to own and drive than the Testa Rossa, which, of course is the successor to this very successful Boxer. I would rate this car as a 10-star and still worth $200,000. Delivered new at the factory in 1984 the price was around $60,000. There is only one acceptable color in this car and that is red with tan interior. More than likely 80% of these cars were made in red. This is a car to collect and own, but be careful to get the papers that show this is a legal car.

1970-1974 246 GT

1. ***** 2. ***** 3. ******* 4. ******

Having covered almost all of the 12-cylinder models, we should concentrate on the 246 Dino. It was and is today a very lovely car with great lines. Also produced by Pininfarina, this little Dino coupe was equipped with a small 2.4 liter V-6 engine in the rear of the car. It was the first rear-engine Ferrari production car to be built. A very light secure feeling was enjoyed by owners of this little coupe. They were not particularly "hot sellers" in the US during the early seventies. The original selling price was around $15,000.

The true Ferrari aficionado never quite accepted this car as a Ferrari. To my knowledge, no Ferrari identification was ever displayed on any exterior badges. Some owners bought the Ferrari chrome logo and installed it at their own discretion. During the late 1980's, this little Dino became quite popular, and was finally "accepted" as a Ferrari. Today it is referred to as a Ferrari Dino. The writer recommends this car to collect and drive with much affection. A very nice coupe is now under $100,000. It certainly will be regarded in the future as one of the great family of Ferraris.

1972-1974   246 GTS Spyder

1. ***** 2. ***** 3. ******** 4. ********

The spyder model was an immediate success. It obviously was a coupe with a "Targa type" roof that could be removed. This made it much more sporty, and it is the most desirable Dino. At the very end of production in 1974, a few hundred cars were built with wide flared fenders and wider wheels which sometimes came with special Daytona style seats. This is the most sought after 246 model, and the value will always be there. Prices today are in the $120,000 to $125,000 range and are quite stable. Obviously, if one in top condition could be purchased close to $100,000, it would represent a good value.

One must be careful to inspect for rust underneath the car and be particularly concerned with rusted-out floors and trunk compartments. The costs of these types of repairs are quite expensive and it may be advisable to start with a "more solid" car that costs more in the beginning, but will not be disappointing as time goes on.

1975-1979   308 GTB-GTS

1. ***** 2. ******* 3. **** 4. *******

The 308 GTB and GTS, as explained earlier in this writing, are extremely satisfying cars to own and drive, but may not be the most desirable to collect because of their sheer numbers of production (approximately 6,000). They did make all of the right "Ferrari noises" from the tailpipe due to the Weber carburetors and minimum early EPA requirements. The clutch on these cars was extremely heavy and one needs to possess a strong left leg. This could be remedied by installation of a later clutch associated with the GTSi models of 1980 and onwards.

It was a basic no-frills Ferrari that was very reliable and fun to drive. There were, as previously stated, a few fiberglass coupes in 1976 that will remain the most collectible of all 308 models. These rarer lightweight coupes are still worth $85,000 and could be real "sleepers" in the future, becoming worth more and more.

1980-1982   308 GTB-GTS

1. ** 2. ** 3. ** 4. **

As can be observed from the rating, this car represents one of the lowest in satisfaction and collectibility of all the Ferrari cars. The engine in this model was fuel injected. As a result of more severe EPA emission requirements, the car really never performed as well as the older 8-cylinder models. It also had a quiet exhaust system. Instead of making all of those lovely Ferrari noises at the tail pipe, the engine sounded as though it were "straining" when asked to perform. This one should be bought cheaper than any other 308 model. At a stop light, don't get into a drag race, because you will be disappointed.

1983-1985   Quattro Valve GTB-GTS

1. ****** 2. ******** 3. ***** 4. ********

In 1983, Ferrari realized that the 2-valve cars of 1980 were not powerful enough and added a 4-valve cylinder head. The result was that this car acted like a true Ferrari. It was the final evolution of the 308. New power, new interior, power door locks and wider wheels made this an extremely successful model. Less than 4,000 of these cars were built, making it difficult to buy in the years produced. Some say that this is the best of the 308 series and I would not disagree. With all of these nice changes being made and the exhaust sounding better, it was fun to drive.

I know of no one at Ferrari who would not recommend this car for ownership experience, and it may prove over time to be a collectible. It is too early to tell what is in the future. It's a good bet that after being so popular when new, the value would carry over into future years. It is truly a fool-proof, low-maintenance, excellent car to drive everyday if you like.

1986-1989 328 GTB-GTS

1.******** 2. ******** 3. ******** 4. ********

Actually, the 328 model was a face-lifted 308 model with integrated bumpers front and rear that were quite pleasing. It tended to round off the corners of the car therefore giving this model a fresh new look. Due to the relatively small numbers of cars that were available during this period of time and at the death of Enzo Ferrari, it was perceived by the customer and enthusiast alike that this would be a collectible car. As it turned out, it was very collectible. Although most people paid all-time high prices for the 328 during 1988 and 1989, they will probably be rewarded for their investment in due time. At the present time, there are not many of these cars on the market.

The 328 was a very pleasing and reliable car to drive. Even though high prices were paid for this model, owners were very satisfied with the quality of the fit and finish as well as with the overall driver feeling of satisfaction. This was the last of the transverse engines and its final refinement. Anyone who owns this car will be happy with it for a long time. The collectibility aspect would therefore be very good. Good cars when new will always make good cars when they are old, thus having real value as well as perceived value. This car rates very high, having scored eight stars in all categories.

We are almost finished with the eight-cylinder Ferraris, but it would be improper not to give some credit to the Mondial which was introduced in 1981 as a 2 + 2 model.

1981-1982   Mondial Coupe

1. **   2. **   3. *   4. **

As you can see, this Mondial coupe was a 2 + 2 (and not a very useful 2 + 2 at that) and it was not a hit. As a 2-valve version it was sluggish, under-powered and not satisfying to drive. It had a pleasant shape, but that is where the satisfaction ended. This car can be purchased fairly reasonably, but does not offer any excitement in return.

1982-1985   Mondial 328 Coupe and Cabriolet

1. **   2. **   3. **   4. *****

In an attempt to make this model more desirable, the 4-valve (Quattrovalve) engine and convertible roof were added. This model enjoyed limited success and was much more acceptable with more power. The availability of a convertible and improved drivability enhanced the collectibility somewhat, and added some strength to this model.

1986-1989 328 Coupe and Cabriolet

1. **   2. ******   3. **   4. *****

To make this car a continuing part of the Ferrari model selection, more power was added with a slight redesign of the interior. As you can see, my feeling of this car is that it is nice to drive and own, but will not have much future collectible value. Used car prices on the cabriolet have held up quite well, however, due to the low numbers that were actually produced in later years.

1985-1987 Testa Rossa 12-Cylinder "Boxer" Coupe

1. ******** 2. ******** 3. ******** 4. **********

After absence from the US market for 11 years, the 12-cylinder Testa Rossa was an immediate success. From the time of its introduction until 1990, a buyer could only hope to be put on a waiting list for possibly 18 months to purchase a car. The Testa Rossa (red head) became so popular that premiums were paid to get the car earlier. Prices started in 1985 at $87,500 and now have reached as high as $176,000 in current form. This is a very powerful, smooth, pleasurable, reliable Ferrari that a tall man can enjoy. It has a roomy cabin and its distinctive styling with giant functional air scoops along the side will be popular for many years to come.

Again, I would add, if it was a hit when it was new, it will be a hit in the future when it will be very collectible. It is very reliable and can run in slow traffic as well as run fast on the open road. The interior looks great, feels great and has good air conditioning and sound system. Currently, the car is priced very reasonably due to the setback in the economy of 1991, and it is as inexpensive as this car will ever be in the future. It is #1 on the Hit Parade!

1988-1989-1990-1991 Testa Rossa Coupe

1. ******** 2. ******** 3. ******** 4. **********

Continued refinements on small items such as rear view mirrors and slight interior features make it a continued favorite, and while the later cars now have bolt on wheels, they are continuing to be the flagship of the Ferrari model line-up. My best advice is for the collector to enjoy this car to drive while it will continue to hold its value and be very collectible.

SUMMARY

Collecting a Ferrari could be the most rewarding thing to do or it could also become a disaster. Look for rust in the body first of all and signs of a prior accident. This requires only the expertise of a good restoration shop with the right intentions to steer you on the right path. Be careful that your adviser is looking out for your best interest and not looking for work for his restoration shop.

My advice here is that it is always better to buy a good car to start with on restoration, because it will end up as a good car. A bad car may not necessarily end up being satisfactory even after a lot of money is spent. Again, the price you pay for an adviser or consultant could save you a lot of money in the long run.

Seek out the advice of your local Ferrari dealer when contemplating any Ferrari purchase. He can advise you if the car has been altered and if it has the proper engine, wheels, etc., and he can tell the difference between a US legal car and a car built for Europe and converted to US specs.. Prior to 1967, there is no worry on this issue, because "Federal" cars were made from 1968 onward and these were the ones subject to modification.

Make sure that if you purchase a 12-cylinder car built from 1974 through 1984 that you know it has proper paperwork and that it has been certified by the DOT and EPA. While the Treasury Department has probably forgotten about the car by this time, it is never safe unless you have the papers. This is also true for other Ferrari models that have not been imported as US versions and are subject to scrutiny.

After you are satisfied that the Ferrari you are looking at passes your test and that of the adviser, you will have to determine whether you are going to drive the car as was intended or are going to "collect."

In the opinion of many of the experts, the market is as depressed as it will ever be, and it would be a good time to step forward (although cautiously) for a collectible car. Many speculators have nice merchandise and must finally unload their cars to pay off notes. The point to be made here is that the market at this time will not support a premium price, so that the car you want will be able to be purchased at realistic value. This value is not at risk in my opinion.

The risk/reward relationship has passed its peak, and has settled down to where it will be for a year or so with values maintaining their purchase price. It is also inevitable that the real collector Ferraris will increase in value over time again, and the most desirable models when new will always be the ones to look for. In order of preference, I would still go with the Daytona and the 512 Boxer. These cars will be sought after forever and there are not enough to go around.

Less than 1,500 Daytona models were made and considerably fewer Boxers were made (about half as many as Daytonas). These cars are among the most desirable of Ferrari models and should prove to be a stable investment. Even for a budget investor, it would be adviseable to stick to a V-12 Ferrari of any kind before venturing out for a V-8 model. There will never be a shortage of V-8 powered cars. They were semi-mass produced, and in two years of production out-numbered all of the cars that were built for the first 20 years of production.

To sum it all up, Ferrari will always be the leader when it comes to collectible imported sports cars. Maserati, Porsche, Lamborghini and Jaguar will always be looking up to Ferrari. The name has magic and its looks and sound will satisfy your investable dollars and make it truly the most satisfying collectible that you can afford. Good hunting!

FERRARI SOURCE REFERENCE GUIDE

Ferrari North America Inc.
250 Sylvan Avenue
Englewood Cliffs, NJ 07632
201-816-2600
Contact: Ken McKay

John Barnes, Jr.
Cavallino Magazine
Box 810819
Boca Raton, FL   33481-0819

Gerald Roush
Roush Publications
Box 870709
Stone Mountain, GA   30087-0018

Ferrari Club of America
9632 SE City View Drive
Portland, OR   97266-6903

Ferrari Owners Club
1708 Seabright Avenue
Long Beach, CA   90813
213-432-9607
Contact: Pat Benz

Ferrari Parts and Information

Algar Enterprises
1234 Lancaster Avenue
Box 167
Rosemont, PA   19010
215-527-1100

Continental Classic Motors
420 East Ogden Avenue
Hinsdale, IL   60521
708-655-3535

FAF Motorcars, Inc.
3862 Stephens Court
Tucker, GA   30084
404-939-5344

Hollywood Sport Cars
5766 Hollywood Boulevard.
Hollywood, CA   90028
213-464-6161

Bill Rudd Motors
14326 Oxnard Street
Van Nuys, CA   91401
818-988-7833

Sheldon Ferrari
5750 North Federal Highway
Fort Lauderdale, FL   33308
305-493-5211

FERRARI RESTORATION SHOPS

Berlinetta Motorcars, Ltd.
138 Railroad Street
Huntington Station, NY 11746
516-423-1010

Coachwork Auto Showcase
9404 West Ogden
Brookfield, IL   60513
708-485-9191
Contact: Steve Campbell

European Auto Restorations, Inc.
1665 Babcock Street
Costa Mesa, CA   92627
714-642-0054

Or contact any authorized Ferrari dealer in your area.

ABOUT THE AUTHOR

John Weinberger was born in 1932 in the back seat of a 1932 Chevy "with gasoline in his veins." He has worked as a Ford mechanic, operated an import repair shop with his brother Herm, dealt Triumph, MG, Jaguar, Toyota, Porsche, DeTomaso, Austin-Healey and Peugeot. During this time, John raced sports cars quite successfully in SCCA until 1969. His racing interest continues today through vintage racing in a Lotus 23B, and his Ferrari collection includes a 288 GTO. In 1975, his Continental Motors was awarded the Ferrari franchise, and today the Hinsdale, Illinois dealership and service facility includes Rolls Royce, Maserati and Lotus.

YEAR	LINE	Relative Condition: Worse ↔ Better		
		❸	❷	❶
1960—1962	250 GT PF Series II Cabriolet	275000	305000	345000
1958—1962	250 GT Pininfarina Coupe	85000	110000	130000
1960—1963	250 GTE 2+2	50000	70000	85000
1962—1964	250 GT Lusso Coupe	245000	270000	315000
1964—1966	275 GTB Coupe	295000	340000	390000
1965—1966	275 GTS Cabriolet	235000	270000	325000
1966—1968	275 GTB/4 Coupe	640000	700000	830000
1964—1968	330 GT MK I/II 2+2	45000	62000	80000
1966—1968	330 GTC Coupe	100000	125000	155000
1966—1968	330 GTS Cabriolet	245000	270000	315000
1968—1969	206 GT Dino Coupe	90000	115000	135000
1968—1970	365 GTC Coupe	160000	195000	240000
1967—1971	365 GT 2+2	65000	90000	110000
1968—1973	365 GTB/4 Coupe	190000	215000	255000
1972—1973	365 GTB/4 Spyder	700000	785000	845000
1970—1974	246 GT Coupe	64000	84000	98000
1972—1974	246 GTS Targa	80000	95000	110000
1971—1972	365 GTC/4 2+2	90000	115000	135000
1974—1976	365 GT4/BB Coupe	160000	180000	205000
1972—1976	365 GT4 2+2	45000	65000	80000
1976—1980	400 Coupe	50000	60000	75000

YEAR	LINE	Relative Condition: Worse ↔ Better		
		❸	❷	❶
1980—1984	400i Coupe	60000	70000	85000
1976—1981	BB512 Coupe	150000	170000	195000
1982—1984	BB512i Coupe	160000	175000	210000
1974—1979	308 GT4 2+2	30000	36000	44000
1978—1979	308 GTS Targa	39000	46000	57000
1975—1979	308 GTB Coupe	38000	44000	55000
1975—1977	308 GTB Fiberglass Coupe	64000	75000	85000
1980—1982	308 GTSi Targa	38000	44000	50000
1980—1982	308 GTBi Coupe	38000	44000	52000
1983—1985	308 GTSi QV Targa	44000	49000	61000
1983—1985	308 GTBi QV Coupe	43000	49000	59000
1985—1989	412 Coupe	70000	86000	105000
1985—1987	Testarossa Coupe	95000	110000	120000
1988—1989	Testarossa Coupe	120000	125000	155000
1981—1982	Mondial 8 2+2	32000	39000	46000
1982—1985	Mondial QV 2+2	36000	44000	52000
1983—1985	Mondial QV Cabriolet	45000	50000	60000
1986—1989	Mondial 3.2 2+2	48000	58000	65000
1986—1989	Mondial 3.2 Cabriolet	55000	62000	70000
1986—1989	328 GTS Targa	62000	70000	78000
1986—1989	328 GTB Coupe	60000	70000	76000

JAGUAR

BY MIKE COOK

A LEGEND AND A LEGENDARY VALUE

It began in a garage behind a modest suburban home in Blackpool, and within ten years was on the way to becoming a legend. When William Lyons, just 21 years old, joined William Walmsley in the manufacture of motorcycle sidecars in the garage behind Walmsley's house, he may have had a dream of becoming an automobile manufacturer but even he, already the astute businessman, could not have dreamed how far the enterprise would go. The year was 1922.

There was some luck in the timing of the formation of the Swallow Sidecar Company because England was prosperous, motorcycles were plentiful and reasonable in cost and, although the "people's car", in the form of the Model T, had arrived in the United States, the affordable Austin Seven and Morris Eight were still several years in England's future. The way for the working man to get around with his wife or girlfriend was on a motorcycle/sidecar combination. Swallow's sleek polished aluminum sidecars were sporty enough for anyone and made to fit the buyer's choice of motorcycle. When the garage became too small, the two partners found space in three different buildings for their initial production but soon again needed larger facilities.

The space was found in downtown Blackpool on Cocker Street during 1926, a year in which William Lyons first envisioned building custom car bodies in addition to the motorcycle sidecars. The first, built on an Austin Seven chassis, was completed during 1927, a tiny little two-seater convertible with a removable hardtop. With engineering modifications being made as cars were produced, these little Austins quickly became popular. The company became the Swallow Sidecar and Coachbuilding Company, in volume production of sedans and convertibles on Morris, Fiat and other chassis as well as Austins. They sold not only to individual buyers but to established car dealers who wanted volume runs delivered on time.

Once again, space was at a premium and this time Walmsley and Lyons knew they had to move from non-industrial seaside Blackpool closer to their sources of supply for chassis and other manufactured parts. They took a giant step to England's industrial heartland and settled in historic Coventry, already a center of British automobile manufacturing.

The factory acquired by Swallow consisted of two large sheds which had been used for filling artillery shells during World War I. Run-down and dilapidated-looking, they were structurally sound and although the floors were wood they were sturdy enough to support a real production line for the lightweight, sporty, Swallow-bodied cars. The plant continued production of the still-popular sidecars and a range of custom-bodied sedans and convertibles but the ambitious Lyons was tiring of modifying other manufacturers' cars and the design limitations that this method imposed. He was corresponding with the General Manager of the Standard Motor Company, John Black, with an exciting new idea in mind. Swallow was already building a successful line of "Standard Swallows" on chassis supplied by Standard and the profits encouraged Black and Lyons to develop a more creative association.

In 1931, this new goal was achieved and the first SS car appeared. Based on a chassis supplied exclusively to Swallow by the Standard Motor Company, the long, low coupe was shown to the public at the London Motor Show in October. The London Daily Express described it as "The Car With The 1000 Pound (Sterling) Look." Actual cost? Just 310 Pounds. Public response to the first complete car built by Swallow was ecstatic. Demand for the car was instant.

The Swallow custom coachwork business continued through 1931 and 1932, winding down to a trickle of cars in 1933. By that time, a new company, SS Cars Ltd., had been formed and Britain's newest car manufacturer was established.

The photos and history of the Swallow-bodied Austins and others are fascinating and inspiring to the collector. Although proper records don't exist, estimates have been made that about 4000 were built, 3500 of which were based on Austin Seven chassis. Rushing out to look for a source of a collectible car will do the enthusiast little good. Almost none of these neat little cars still exist. A few Austins, one Swift, one Standard, a Wolseley, are all that remains to show what the enthusiast on a tight budget could buy to be "different" in the late 'twenties and early 'thirties. Like other rare models from the period, they are difficult to value and may be less interesting than the volume production XK and E Type Jaguar sports models built 20 years or more later. This is due in part to lack of knowledge among collectors and also to the fact that it can be less interesting to own a rare car about which few other collectors know anything. The possessor of such a car loses out on a lot of bull sessions at car shows.

Although Swallow sidecars were built for many years, few of those remain, testifying to the relatively low production. A smart example graces Jaguar's museum in Coventry.

For the collector in pursuit of a William Lyons product, the SS range offers more hope and variety. Production of these cars was small by comparison with many of the world's famous marques. Yet they commanded extraordinary interest from the motoring press and the car-buying public for three reasons which are still the foundation of Jaguar's success: styling, performance and value for money.

SS Cars Ltd. was incorporated in 1933. In 1934, the new firm was awarded a stand in the manufacturers' area at the London Motor Show for the first time, having previously held space in the coachbuilders section. That November, William Walmsley left the company and William Lyons was in sole control of SS! In business for only 12 years, the company had reached astonishing heights of fame, had increased its business year after year, straight through the Depression years and was going strong.

To strengthen SS financially and provide for the future of the growing business, Lyons took the company public in January of 1935 and demand for the shares was excellent. A separate company was formed to continue the still-active sidecar business.

If asked, a car enthusiast of the day might have said that Lyons and SS Cars had "made it". The company was producing a high-performance line of cars with a world reputation at very reasonable prices and it looked as though its success would continue. Yet, William Lyons had something else in the back of his mind; a name, a stronger identity for his products. From a broad choice he selected Jaguar.

The choice of Jaguar as the name for the already-famous SS line of cars was the major publicity item for the company that year. However, another 1935 event would be of similar long-term benefit. In April, William M. Heynes was hired to become the company's first chief engineer. He would wield a powerful and effective influence for nearly forty years.

The first SS Jaguar cars were displayed in the autumn of 1935 at the London Motor Show. They were 1936 models and, although some SS1 and SS2 cars were built in 1936, the world now knew the marque as SS Jaguar.

The list of models produced under the SS marque includes two separate ranges of cars in several body styles. The original SS1 was a coupe and only coupes were produced in 1932. In the 1933-36 period, two-door sedans, four-seat tourers, drop-head (convertible) coupes and the Airline fast-back sedan were also built. Just twenty-four examples of the SS 90 two-seater sports car were produced in 1935 and 1936. All of these were built on chassis supplied by the Standard Motor Company and were powered with Standard six-cylinder engines of 2054 or 2552 cc displacement. Prices were all below 400 Pounds Sterling. The SS 90 chassis were shortened to SS2 wheelbase.

In the SS2 range, only coupes were initially available in 1932 and 33. These really tiny cars had a four-cylinder flat-head engine of only 1006 cc and although attractively styled were not great performers. In 1934, SS2s changed dramatically in both horsepower and dimensions. Adopting 1343 and 1608cc Standard engines and larger Standard chassis, SS2 sedans and tourers were added to the coupe style. These cars could accommodate driver and passengers more readily and carry them at more normal highway speeds.

However, the SS2 range accounted for only 1796 vehicles compared to 4254 SS1s. Survivors are few in both series, but examples of all models do exist including at least one each of the original SS2 coupe in the early "helmet-wing" front fender style and the later 1933 version with front fenders (wings) fairing into running boards. The larger SS1 models are well represented including a fine example in the Jaguar Cars collection known as the "Lady Lyons car". Although Lyons is known not to have cared for the Airline model, several good examples exist and are real attention-getters.

Estimating value is difficult with these cars, given the small number existing. However, one SS2 coupe in fully restored condition sold for over $40,000 in the mid-1980s. Minimum asking price for any fully-restored SS1 would be in the $30,000 to $60,000 range with rarities like the SS90 running into six figures. Acquiring one of the SS line will be a difficult enterprise, but worth it, and not completely impossible in terms of obtaining parts. There are registers for all of these pre-war SS cars and an active group of collectors in, for example, the Classic Jaguar Association in the United States. Restoration of the coach-built bodies is expensive and often requires virtually reproducing the body and its underlying ash wood frame. Although many of the engines were built by Standard for their own cars as well as for SS Cars, there is a problem, for example, in obtaining replacement cylinder heads.

The small volume of SS production in the 1930s dictated that there would be carry-over SS models built in 1936 and transitional SS Jaguars sharing characteristics and left-over parts from the pure SS of 1935. Tourer bodies, for example, were made as SS Jaguars in virtually the same style as the 1934 and 1935 SS units. A very few early SS Jaguar tourers had the flat-head 2552 cc engines, but the balance shared the "new" sixes with Weslake-designed overhead-valve heads. These engines of 2664 cc and 1776 cc displacement, were still built for SS by Standard. At the bottom of the range was a sedan powered by the old 1608 cc flathead four.

In the 1936 SS Jaguar range appeared the first four-door "saloon" to be produced by Lyons' company. The graceful lines were shared (or copied) by other makes of the period but none were better proportioned. The initial 1936 offerings were the four-door, tourer and, most exciting, the "100" sports two-seater. A genuine, competitive sports car, the SS Jaguar 100 easily matched other marques of the day in performance, although only 314 were produced in four years. Its rakish and beautifully proportioned styling was unequalled and the car remains a very desirable collector's item. It is easily a $200,000 plus investment.

1938 Jaguar SS100

Jaguar Photo

Lyons never let a year go by without adding something significant to his line of cars. In 1936 it was the SS100 and the four-door. In 1937 he made a revolutionary move. The company began production of all-steel bodied SS Jaguars. Although carefully shaped pieces of ash were still to be found, especially in the SS100, growing demand for SS products made modern production lines and welded steel bodies the only solution. At that year's Motor

Show, 3 1/2-liter engines were announced, giving the company a range of 1 1/2 (1776 cc), 2 1/2 (2664 cc) and 3 1/2-liter sedans. Only the two larger engines were available in the SS100. The 1 1/2 was now an overhead-valve unit and shared the same body as the more powerful Jaguars but with a shorter hood. Also in 1938 the tourer was dropped from the line in favor of the four-seat drophead (convertible) with its smarter lines and better weather protection.

The change to the all-steel bodywork had proved expensive and had delayed production, so the company's 1938 financial results did not show the level of growth investors had come to expect. However, a profit was made and, at the Motor Show, a unique two-seater sports coupe, on the SS100 chassis, was shown. Only the prototype was made, although a price was quoted and it may have been planned to produce the car.

This special sportster survives today in the collection of Bob Cole outside San Francisco. It is beautifully restored and the sleek styling both typifies its year of origin and predicts events of a decade later. The front of the car with the huge headlamps and the radiator grille set well back between the bulbous front fenders mark it as a 'thirties machine. At the rear, however, the enthusiast will find it is easy to see the look-to-be of the 1948 XK-120.

The 1940 SS Jaguar models shown at Olympia in October, 1939, were the last pre-World War Two Lyons products. They featured standard equipment such as "air conditioning", actually a heating and ventilation system, the availability of a radio installation and hydraulic shock absorbers on the 3 1/2-liter models. SS had built 5000 cars during 1939, the peak year of pre-war production.

In technical terms, the SS Jaguar line was in the upper middle of European technology. Brakes were mechanical but, with the huge 14-inch drums used, were effective. Engines were state-of-the-art overhead-valve type and the aluminum heads were advanced in design. The car's overall and class-wins in many major European rallies, including the RAC and Monte Carlo, are ample illustration of its handling and performance. Genuine 90 mph sedans were not common in the 'thirties and Jaguar's acceleration and speed were in a high bracket. Instrumentation and standard equipment were at the luxury level and the buyer had many options in equipment, color, etc., often installed at Jaguar's own Customer Service Department.

The collector who takes the time to research availability will be able to find a selection of SS Jaguars. Rarest, perhaps, is the 1936 4-cylinder sedan with its unique bodywork, appearing as a scale model of the larger cars. Also rare are the drop-heads and SS100s, but all can be found. They share the restoration problems of any sixty-year-old car: rust, wood rot, missing equipment, crystallized pot metal castings, etc. However, such is the interest in Jaguars of all kinds that many parts have been reproduced, both metal and rubber, and sources can be found.

Prices quoted are $30,000 to $50,000 for the sedans, up to $100,000 for the drop-heads and $200,000 plus for SS90 and SS100. A big plus for many collectors is that these cars can be driven safely and reliably on the road and, with the possible exception of the 1 1/2 model, have no problem keeping up and stopping with today's traffic. Any pre-war SS or SS Jaguar will be an asset to the collector.

Without World War II, the progress of SS Jaguar might have been more rapid. Knowing the advances in engineering the company had made during its first 18 years in business, this would seem to be a safe prediction. However, the War did happen and, by the end of 1940, whatever cars that had been on the line in the autumn of 1939 had been built and sold and SS was in wartime production mode.

Initially, Lyons had to hustle for war-time contracts to keep his company in business. However, he ended up with a diverse package including construction of thousands of military-style sidecars, bomber repair, construction of amphibious trailers and experimental projects on small Jeep-like vehicles intended to be dropped by parachute. There were also endless hours of air-raid watch duty for everyone, regardless of position and many of these, so it is said, were spent by Lyons and engineers Heynes and Walter Hassan, discussing post-war projects.   From these late-night sessions grew the plans for Jaguar's postwar growth.   One plan was carried out before war ended. From Standard, Lyons acquired the tooling for the 2 1/2 and 3 1/2-liter engines, making it possible for him to start post-war production of his own engines. Only the four-cylinder unit was still made for Jaguar by Standard.

At war's end, in March, 1945, at an extraordinary meeting of the Board, the name of the company was changed to "Jaguar Cars Ltd." Wartime atrocities associated with the SS initials had made the change necessary and William Lyons entered the post-war period at the head of a new company bearing the name he had chosen himself, ten years earlier. The sidecar part of the business had been sold in 1944 so if he was to continue to make history, it would have to be on four wheels. For Lyons, that was no problem.

When production resumed in the fall of 1945, Jaguar's stock in trade consisted of the three pre-war sedans, carried over to make the return to normalcy as easy as possible. Although drop-heads reappeared in 1948 and 1949, the SS100 would not be made again. Those wartime, midnight skull sessions between Lyons and his engineers would pay off dramatically at Earls Court when the XK 120 would be the star of Britain's first post-war motor show.

Only 12,000 of the pre-war styled cars left the Jaguar factory for sale in world markets in the 1946-49 model years.   Virtually identical to their 1930s forebears, they remained high on the list of the world's "performance" cars, and the low volume was well behind the actual orders.   In this period, Jaguar also began a serious export drive. Like all British manufacturers, they were pressured by the government to export or face losing supplies of sheet steel for bodies.   Thus, strong efforts were made to sell Jaguars in Europe and, in 1948, a United States distributor organization was created. Because of this, finding a post-war Jaguar sedan in the United States is somewhat easier than with earlier models. Prices are similar with the drophead again at the top and much rarer than the sedans.

The leading candidate to produce revenue in export markets was the XK 120 and the United States was the primary target. The American market was car-starved and British imports from little Austin and Morris sedans to Standard roadsters and, of course, the MG-TC, all seemed to sell well for a while.

Jaguar sedans and dropheads found a market but it was the two-seater "fun-car" enthusiasm, created mainly by the MG, which opened the USA to Lyons. The XK 120 simply took over the news coverage of the 1948 motor show, and it was quickly obvious as orders rolled in from the USA that the original production estimates were incredibly low. The early cars were aluminum bodied with much hand work but that method was quickly dropped in favor of proper steel bodywork and faster production.

1951 Jaguar XK-120   *Jaguar Photo*

The XK 120 was first an exercise in styling. Lyons' eye for proportion and feel for what would be popular was again accurate in this car. Under the hood (the British still call it a "bonnet") rested another achievement in both engineering and styling. Born of the wartime planning sessions, the XK engine had twin overhead cams and put out 160 brake horsepower. It retained the iron block/aluminum head configuration of the previous Jaguar engines, and was among the most up-to-date powerplants in the automotive world. Furthermore, it looked good. Polished alloy components and ribbed cam covers with the name Jaguar contributed to the look Lyons demanded in all of his cars.

The XK 120 was the first in a series of XK designated sports cars from Jaguar, all having the XK twin-cam six in displacements of 3.4, 3.8 or 4.2 liters. The 120 was indeed a sports car, but, despite the side curtains and rudimentary top on the popular roadster version, it was comfortable, generally weather tight and generations ahead of the cart-sprung SS 100.

Part of the XK 120's easy (by 1948 standards) ride was the comfortable seating. However, in company with the Mark Five sedan, which had been launched a couple of months earlier, the new XK had independent front suspension. Jaguar, like Ford, now its parent, clung to a solid front axle right through 1948, then adopted a Bill Heynes-designed independent system with torsion bars rather than springs. As we have noted before, Lyons often dealt in "giant steps".

The Mark Five, introduced in September of 1948 and equipped with many features of its own, was partially eclipsed by the massive publicity surrounding the XK 120. It was, however, a remarkably good car and a worthy successor to the 1946-48 sedans which essentially carried 1937 engineering into the post-war years.

The Mark Five was the last Jaguar to use the OHV 2 1/2 and 3 1/2-liter and to have the flowing body lines of the pre-war Lyons cars. Today, at first, it appears to be merely a look-alike to its immediate predecessors but actually is vastly more modern. Like the XK 120, the Mark Five has independent front suspension with torsion bars and tubular hydraulic shocks, and thus was the first Jaguar so equipped. The brakes are hydraulic, again a first for Jaguar, with twelve-inch drums all round. The wheels are sixteen inch, down from eighteen.

Styling touches on the Mark Five included thinner windscreen pillars and rear fender "spats" (skirts). To go with an overall larger and heavier appearance compared to the previous models, it had double-channel, very heavy-looking bumpers, expressly for the American market. This final example of traditional British 'thirties styling lasted three years until Jaguar brought out its first sedan without separate fenders, the large, graceful, envelope-bodied Mark Seven.

"Mark Five" as a model designation was a non-sequitur for Jaguar, as there had been no Mark One, Two, Three or Four. The confusion caused by this whimsical designation has been partly eased by the posthumous naming of the 1945-48 cars as "Mark Four". They are now universally known this way but the purist will point out that Jaguar did not so name them. And, although the numbers had reached Mark Seven, there was never a Mark Six.

As collector's items, Mark Five Jaguars are to be found in the pages of various car collector publications. Parts availability and prices are similar to the other 2 1/2 and 3 1/2- liter sedans and availability in the United States is better due to the number imported. These cars also have a steady value to collectors.

Though the XK 120 was as modern as anything on the road, the traditional Mark Five had to be replaced to bring Jaguar into line with postwar automotive design. This was accomplished in the autumn of 1950 when the Jaguar Mark Seven sedan starred at the Earls Court Motor Show in London. To British motorists unused to the large-scale automobiles available in the United States, the Mark Seven must have appeared enormous. Yet, at a little over 16 feet in length, it was just right for the USA and the orders showed it. The all-new car used the well-proven 3.4-liter 160 BHP twin-cam XK engine and was an honest 100-MPH machine. The sleek styling featured the same type of sweeping sculptured line on the body side as the XK 120. On the streamlined sedan, the line suggested the Jaguar heritage of swooping front fender line tying into running board and swelling up again at the rear to form the rear fender shape. Trunk room in the Mark Seven was enormous and passenger accommodations very comfortable. The handling and power were sufficient to make it a successful racing and rally competitor, but it was a highway cruiser from the word go.

The Mark Five was discontinued during 1951. The Mark Seven gained an automatic transmission in 1953. Success in racing helped keep Jaguar's performance reputation up to date with victories at Le Mans in 1951 and 1953 by the "C" Type racer based on the 120. Keeping up with the market, the 120 was upped to 140 in 1954 with the same basic body concealing new rack and pinion steering. Although similar in size and drive train, the XK 150 had all-new styling when it appeared at the end of 1956 and had disc brakes on the front. All of these sportsters were offered in three models: roadster (side curtains and skimpy top), drop-head (roll-up windows and padded top) and coupe. On the 120, the coupe was a two-seater. The later cars had tiny back seats which were bearable for children on short trips.

A similar process of evolution was applied to the big sedan, which became the Mark Eight with one-piece windshield, a chrome styling line on the side which provided for two-tone paint treatment if desired, and the higher horsepower engine designated "M". Later, in 1959, it became the Mark Nine featuring disc brakes and even higher horsepower. Part of the reason for the additional power was an increase in engine size from 3.4 to 3.8 liters. Available in the 150 and Mark Nine, this engine was only another of many displacements created on the basic twin-cam XK engine.

Looking at the various XK sports cars it is easy to demonstrate the features needed to make a car interesting to the collector. Smart appearance first. Then performance, not just horsepower, but handling and braking as well. The car has to be fun to drive; a sports car is, by definition, exciting on the road. From the coupe versions at around $50,000 for a show-standard car, to the roadsters which top $75,000, they are excellent collector cars. They are also tough enough to drive regularly and hard. Many are raced in vintage events. Most reasonably price are the coupes and rarest are the drop-head 120 and 140.

During the exciting 1950s, when William Lyons' company was going from success to success with each new model, another accolade was awarded. The sidecar builder from Blackpool became Sir William Lyons, Knighted by Queen Elizabeth in 1956.

With the sports car range and large, luxury segment covered, Jaguar could look for expansion into another lucrative sales area, the high-speed executive car. In 1959, Lyons used up another of the missing "Mark" numbers and announced what would be called the Mark Two. This sporting four-door sedan with very high performance and dashing, up-to-the-minute styling represented the developing concept of the "personal car", later to be exploited by many manufacturers. The idea was not completely original with Jaguar but they were the first company to do the treatment on a volume production model. In early 2.4-liter and later 3.4, 3.8 and 4.2 forms, the car was a hit!

To be perfectly correct, the original small sedan was simply called the "2.4" and the second model the "3.4". These cars had bodies that tapered sharply inwards at the rear and were "crab-tracked", the front track being four inches wider than the rear. This, and the rather thick windshield and door pillars which obstructed vision and made the car look somewhat heavy, was corrected for 1960 when the actual "Mark Two" came on the market. The slimmed-down pillars gave the revised car a light and airy look and the wider rear track and altered bodywork appeared better aesthetically and gave more trunk room.

Several variations will be seen on the basic Mark Two theme. The 3.8S, introduced in 1964, was the first departure from the overall styling. While basically retaining the normal Mark Two front, it has quite different rear styling, patterned after the large Mark Ten sedan which had gone into production in 1962. The effect is as though two styling teams had worked on the car, at different ends, without communicating. As a road car, however, the S was quite a departure, because it had the independent rear suspension first installed by Jaguar on the legendary E Type in 1961. After the 3.8S came the 420. This time, the front styling matched the rear, and the car was powered by the final version of the XK engine having 4.2 liters displacement. Production ended in 1968.

The most distinctive feature of the small Jaguar sedans was the monocoque construction. The unit body/chassis was made by Pressed Steel Fisher in Oxford. It was extremely rigid and well-made but prone to rusting, especially in North America. These smaller Jaguars did not suffer for lack of luxury. The wood panelling equalled both the quality and the area of the Mark 7 - 9 series. Leather was omnipresent, instrumentation complete and equipment comprehensive. For example, automatic transmission, power steering and real air conditioning were available and the larger-displacement models could reach 130 MPH! They were in every way the world's first high-performance "compact" luxury sedans. Current collector publications show the 3.8 Mark Two near $50,000 for a concours quality car while the 420, offered only in 1967-68, is a sleeper at under $20,000. The collector can expect the cars to hold value but they can't be expected to reach the dollar level of the popular sports Jaguars.

The Mark Two body was the first Jaguar design to be modified into a Daimler. Jaguar had purchased the traditional and conservative Daimler Company in 1960. The new small car offered a perfect platform for the 2 1/2-liter Daimler V8 which Americans had seen in the Daimler SP-250 sports car. Thus, in 1962, small Jaguar-bodied cars with fluted grilles, a burbling exhaust and a curly D badge on the grille and wheel centers began to appear. These cars, mostly automatics, were not sold in the United States, although some, usually right-hand drive, have found their way here. Last of the series, the 420-bodied Daimlers, were named "Sovereign", a name much used by Jaguar since. They are usually very reasonably priced and have all the looks and features of the Jaguar versions.

The small-bodied sedans from Jaguar are readily available. The buyer must know his stuff regarding rust because the monocoques were not well rust-proofed, and most have rotted in one place or more. Body panels can be replaced or repaired, but the task can be considerable if the rust has gained a big foothold. Such is their popularity that at least one restoration firm in England offers a virtually new Mark Two, which can have a modern 5-speed transmission and other up-rated features, all at very high cost.

Now, having covered the Executive Express, we need to backtrack to look at two other Jaguar lines that were offered beginning in the 1960s; the E-Type or XKE and the Mark Ten sedan, Jaguar's largest car, launched in 1961 and 1962, respectively. They were significant in many ways but, primarily, the E-Type was the last true Jaguar sports car, and the Mark Ten the last Jaguar sedan prior to Jaguar's most important and successful series, the XJ sedans.

By 1960, the XK series of Jaguar sports cars had lost momentum in the market. Under the sleek XK 150 body there was still a 1948 chassis and something more modern was needed. Jaguar's racing success of the 1950s had been accomplished with the C and D Types, both of which made significant contributions to production car development. From the C Type came disc brakes. From the D came the E Type styling which endures three decades later as one of the most appealing automotive designs ever conceived.

Tested through the late 1950s, the E Type line was seen in races in both Europe and the United States where prototypes were entered by Briggs Cunningham. The refined result of much testing in competition and on the road was introduced in 1961 at Geneva and New York. Press and public reaction was, if anything, more enthusiastic than for the XJK 120. Although E Type was the official designation, the car was promoted in the United States as "XKE".

The envelope-bodied E Type was announced in both coupe and "roadster" form. However, the traditional roadster side curtains were gone and roll-up windows graced both models. The coupe styling was superb with not a line out of place and the soft-top looked good even with top up! Powered by the 3.8-liter XK gold-head engine which had previously been available in the "S" version of the XK 150, the E Type was a genuine 150 MPH car but replete with grand touring amenities. All-independent suspension, the first for Jaguar, comfortable seating, traditional Jaguar leather interior (although the E did not share the woodwork of its predecessors) and top-quality body and paint work. A few all or part-aluminum "lightweights" were offered for owners interested in competition, and one of these scored a first place at Oulton Park in April, 1961, just a few months after the E Type was launched.

1968 Jaguar XKE 2+2　　　　　　　　　　　　　　　　　　*Jaguar Photo*

E Types were the sports car of choice in the upper price bracket for many years. Introduced in the USA at about $4000 for the roadster, they were excellent value and their looks drew attention everywhere. The first modifications of significance were made in 1964 when the car received a new gearbox, replacing the elderly Moss-manufactured unit with no first gear synchromesh, and the 4.2-liter engine. Two years later, a 2+2 coupe was added which had automatic available. 1968 saw further body mods to suit US safety regulations, including full bumpers, altered headlight positioning and raised parking lights. A larger grille opening provided sufficient cooling to allow air conditioning to be offered. These were the "Series II" E Types.

Development of Jaguar's famous all-aluminum V12 engine had progressed to the point by 1970 that it was ready to be installed into a car. The E Type was selected and, in 1971, the Series III E was announced. Built on the longer wheelbase of the 2+2, this E was offered only as a roadster and a 2+2. Performance was back up near the 150 MPH range and acceleration with either manual or automatic was brilliant. This was the biggest and most comfortable of the Es and was handsome with top up or down. It also had the only actual grille ever featured on the series. Previous Es had a plain opening or a slim bar with central badge. The V12 had wider track and flared wheel arches, giving it a more massive look. The XK designation disappeared along with the venerable six and the car was called "Series III E Type V12", still a mouthful.

Hard to believe again, these remarkable performers were becoming a hard sell by 1973 and the final year of production was 1974. A run of 50 commemorative roadsters was made, 49 black and one racing green and these went to collectors at high prices. The final unit resides in Jaguar's museum. The United States had ordered an extra run of 1974 models which were sold during 1975 while the company waited for the next sporting Jaguar model. Not a true sports car but a genuine grand tourer, the XJS would arrive as a 1976 model.

The E Type experience for the collector can be very rewarding. Nearly 73,000 were made and large numbers have been preserved. Even so, the number of high quality survivors is not great due to pernicious rust and the car's vulnerability to damage from larger cars. The top end of the market hit astronomical heights in the late 1980s with prices for the V12 roadsters shooting well over $100,000. This has settled down and current figures are more realistic. Prices are higher outside the United States and there has been a steady flow of E types of all models back to England and Europe and across the Pacific to Far Eastern collections.

Locating an E-Type in the USA is still relatively easy and all models are available, often in the normal newspaper classified. The buyer needs to look for matching features to be certain the car is not assembled from parts of several Es and can take advantage of Jaguar's Vehicle Data service which will advise what color and equipment were on the car when it was built and confirm the numbers of chassis engine, gearbox, etc. Least desirable are the six cylinder 2+2s which are also the least attractive, bringing no more than $30,000 for a concours machine. The V12 roadster is at the top with high quality cars bringing close to $ 100,000 in Europe where they are more rare. As a long-term investment the E Type is very desirable. For the collector who likes to drive his cars it is a rewarding car on the road, capable of out-running many modern cars although a bit deficient in the brake department.

During the profitable 1960s, Sir William Lyons was looking at his retirement and planning for the future of Jaguar. He engineered a merger with British Motor Corporation, carried out in 1966, which he believed would guarantee Jaguar, as a small firm, the technical and financial resources to carry on in the increasingly competitive world auto market. He could not foresee that his financially sound company would be dragged down by losses created by BMC and that a further merger with the Leyland Motor Corporation would create British Leyland in 1968. This conglomerate, intended to preserve the British car industry, came close to killing it. Jaguar survived only through some adroit, behind-the-scenes, management moves.

Jaguar also survived, once again, through well-designed, magnificently engineered, timely products. Through the 1970s and 1980s a new series of Jaguars, the XJ models, kept the company going.

1980 Jaguar XJ6   *Jaguar Photo*

First announced was the XJ6. Successor to both the big 420G, last of the Mark Ten line and the small 420 which ended the Mark Two range, the XJ6 incorporated all the successful elements of those cars into a new medium-sized unit body-chassis with virtually timeless styling which would be produced for more than 20 years.

The 4.2-liter XK engine, Jaguar's incredibly smooth four-wheel independent suspension, a roomy passenger compartment finished in leather with walnut trim, full instrumentation, luxury equipment including power windows and brakes, automatic, air conditioning, etc. was Lyons' standard Jaguar prescription for sales success. However, the XJ6 combination was something very special. It was a truly modern car which sacrificed nothing in handling and road performance. The basic car evolved into a range with the arrival of the long-wheelbase "L" model in 1971 and V12 powered versions, dubbed XJ12, in the same year. A Series II with fuel injection and revised front end styling arrived in 1973 and very smart hardtop coupes, named XJ6C and 12C were built in 1974-78. These were on the short wheelbase but the long variant was standardized on the four doors starting with the Series II. Daimler variants were built in all of these styles with little change other than interior appointments and badging. These were marketed primarily in the UK.

The final XJ with the XK engine was the Series III. Introduced during 1979, it carried on through 1987 in six-cylinder form, and is still being built as a 12-cylinder, although not for the USA. One of the best reworks ever of an existing car, this Jaguar has ideal proportions, lots of glass area, and by the time it came along, offered a "traditional" choice to buyers of luxury cars. It went out of production on the launch of the "new XJ6", an all-new sedan that was introduced in 1986. A few hundred V12 Series IIIs are now built each year.

The second XJ Jaguar was the XJS, introduced in the fall of 1975. Powered by the V12, this 2+2 coupe was equal in size to the four-door but with a completely different body having very American styling. Inside there were leather seats but the dash was plastic rather than wood and the instruments were more like

Detroit than Coventry.

1982 Jaguar XJS *Jaguar Photo*

Underneath, the XJS had the Jaguar independent suspension, automatic transmission, etc., but it was a heavy touring sedan, not a sports car, and it got off to a slow start. Without any styling or other change through 1980, sales were declining to hundreds, rather than thousands, and production was suspended until the 1982 HE model could be readied.

The HE, for High Efficiency, had modified cylinder heads which gave more power and better economy. The interior now had elm veneer trim, styling details including new wheels gave a smarter appearance and the car was finished nicely. Sales curved upward. A Cabriolet (XJSC) with removable roof panels was launched in 1984 and a full convertible replaced the XJSC in 1988. A sporting coupe with six-cylinder power and a 5-speed gearbox is currently offered in Europe and the company forecasts that the XJS will remain in the line for the foreseeable future. It is often seen at club concours events and the pre-1982 models are often good buys at around $ 10,000 or less. The buyer should determine that the car is in good mechanical condition, as the engine and drive train components, while sturdy, are very expensive to repair. Fuel injection components are subject to failure as is the electronic ignition.

XJ6 sedans from 1968 through 1987 are popular collector cars and remain at popular prices as well. Only the relatively rare two-door hardtops will reach $20,000 and then only if in 100 point condition. 12- cylinder cars are rarer in the United States because, although Series I and II V12s were imported in quantity, only about 35 Series IIIs were brought in, during 1979, before the company dropped them to achieve a better Corporate Average Fuel Economy rating. The later Series IIIs are still in the normal used car market and excellent examples can be found.

In the 1970s, Jaguar's fortunes, as part of British Leyland, were at a low point. Product quality dropped and the organization was absorbed into BL to the point where only the Engineering Department remained a Jaguar entity. Sir Michael Edwardes, chairman of BL, recognized the value of Jaguar as a marque and hired John Egan, in 1980, to revive the company. Under Egan, the Series III became a best seller and the various XJS HE models were developed. From 1984 through 1989, Jaguar became an independent company again, as Jaguar plc, and the shares were among the most active on both London and New York exchanges. The firm's fortunes again ebbed with the decline in the value of the dollar against the Pound Sterling. Egan sought a partner. In December, 1989, Jaguar was purchased by Ford and is now a wholly-owned subsidiary of Ford of England.

Part of the reason for Jaguar's financial problems was the huge investment required to bring the new XJ6 to market. Conceived as a new platform to carry Jaguar through the 1990s, the car did not carry over any components from the Series III. It incorporated a new all-aluminum 3.6-liter engine, ZF automatic, new suspension, computer-controlled electronic systems and so many different items that production quality dipped seriously in the 1987, 1988 and 1989 model years. The expenditure required to bring the cars up to Jaguar quality standards was too much to handle,and Ford's interest was very welcome.

Interestingly enough, the latest sedans, which are often referred to by the factory code name XJ40, are already popular entries at concours d'elegance and seem likely to help Jaguar collecting enthusiasm continue. However, the lack of a sports model in the line has turned Jaguar into a purveyor of high-priced cars for the wealthy and, even though they still represent excellent value, only a few can afford them. It is hoped that the built-in quality and traditional features will attract the collector in future. Current used-car values can be seen in the regular classified and good buys can be found in 1988 and 89 models. Jaguar used car values hold up more firmly than they did in the 60s and 70s.

Longevity has become a trademark of Jaguar. The XJ6 sedan range and the XJS models now being built were developed early enough to be evaluated before production by Sir William Lyons, who died in 1985. The company is predicting several new ranges of cars to be built by the end of the century but severe marketing challenges face it as competition in the luxury field grows. It will be up to the dedication of the management and the Ford Motor Company to ensure that Jaguar cars remain what they are today, that is, uniquely styled, distinctive luxury cars with a built-in tradition of performance that is the legacy of Bill Lyons from Blackpool.

INFORMATION SOURCES

Jaguar Clubs of North America
555 MacArthur Blvd.
Mahwah, N.J. 07430-2327

JCNA has 50 affiliates in the United States and offers a full range of member services including the JAGUAR JOURNAL, a bi-monthly magazine, and individual pamphlets on specific Jaguar models and other items. Local affiliates offer social and competitive events, annual national competitions in concours, rallying and other events.

Jaguar Archive
c/o Jaguar Cars Inc.
555 MacArthur Blvd.
Mahwah, N.J. 07430-2327

The Jaguar Archive offers research services for a fee. It is the only
source for North American owners of original data on all SS, Jaguar
and Daimler cars as recorded at the factory. Technical information,
literature and other material is catalogued. Write or call for
information.

The Classic Jaguar Association
26045 Rotunda Drive
Carmel, CA 93923

CJA offers the collectors of XK and earlier Jaguar and SS Cars a
regular publication and sources of information and parts. The
association also has an excellent library. Associated with JCNA.

ABOUT THE AUTHOR

Mike Cook's first ride in a sports car was in a Jaguar XK-120 at age
16. Already a car nut, from then on he was a confirmed British
sports car enthusiast. After college, he worked in the auto
business, becoming PR manager for British Leyland in 1968. As
Jaguar was one of the British marques under BL's banner, Mike
began a life-long association with Jaguar. Driving and learning
about all the cars was part of the job. Becoming knowledgeable
about the earlier cars took somewhat longer, and involved Mike
with Jaguar Clubs of North America, of which he is now president.
He has authored books and magazine articles, and edited the
Jaguar Journal, magazine of the JCNA.

YEAR	LINE	Relative Condition: Worse ↔ Better		
		❸	❷	❶
1952—1954	XK-120M Roadster	45000	60000	72000
1952—1954	XK-120M Coupe	24000	30000	37000
1949—1954	XK-120 Roadster	35000	45000	58000
1951—1954	XK-120 Coupe	19000	27000	33000
1953—1954	XK-120 Drop Head	32000	42000	56000
1955—1957	XK-140 Roadster	35000	45000	57000
1955—1957	XK-140 Drop Head	34000	44000	56000
1955—1957	XK-140 Coupe	20000	27000	33000
1955—1957	XK-140 MC Coupe	22000	30000	36000
1955—1957	XK-140 MC Roadster	39000	50000	72000
1955—1957	XK-140 MC Drop Head	38000	48000	66000
1958—1961	XK-150 Coupe	19000	26000	32000
1959—1961	XK-150 Roadster	40000	49000	62000
1958—1961	XK-150 Drop Head	31000	40000	50000
1958—1961	XK-150 S Coupe	23000	30000	37000
1959—1961	XK-150 S Roadster	42000	53000	70000

YEAR	LINE	Relative Condition: Worse ↔ Better		
		❸	❷	❶
1958—1961	XK-150 S Drop Head	40000	50000	65000
1961—1964	XKE Series I Roadster	34000	41000	50000
1961—1964	XKE Series I Coupe	18000	28000	36000
1965—1967	XKE Series I Roadster	28000	36000	47000
1965—1967	XKE Series I Coupe	16000	24500	34000
1966—1967	XKE Series I 2+2	16500	23000	32000
1967—1968	XKE Series 1.5 Roadster	25000	34000	40000
1967—1968	XKE Series 1.5 Coupe	14000	21000	27000
1967—1968	XKE Series 1.5 2+2	12500	20000	25000
1969—1971	XKE Series II Roadster	25000	31000	41000
1969—1971	XKE Series II Coupe	14000	21000	27000
1969—1971	XKE Series II 2+2	13500	21000	27000
1972—1974	XKE Series III Roadster	35000	43000	57000
1971—1974	XKE Series III 2+2	15500	21000	31000
1975—1976	XJ6 C Coupe	8500	12000	17000
1975—1976	XJ12 C Coupe	10000	15000	19000

LAMBORGHINI

BY JIM KAMINSKI

THE MAN AND THE CAR

Automobili Ferruccio Lamborghini, SpA was launched into sports car production with the introduction of its 350GTV show car at the Turin Auto Show on October 30, 1963.

The creator of this radical marque was Ferruccio Lamborghini, the Italian tractor magnate. Born in northern Italy on April 28, 1916, he grew up in a farming environment. His early interests inclined toward motors and mechanical things. Therefore, his parents sent him to an industrial college in nearby Bologna, where he earned an industrial engineering degree. Shortly after he graduated, World War II began, and he was drafted into the army.

Serving in a transportation pool on the island of Rhodes, Lamborghini earned a reputation for innovative repairs on military equipment. Spare parts were scarce, so he learned to improvise with whatever was available to him. This experience honed his skills as an entrepreneur for his successes yet to come.

After the war, he returned home to set up a small garage and tuning business. He modified Fiats for racing, gaining somewhat of a reputation. He tried driving but found he didn't have the exceptional ability required. His attention turned to servicing a post-war need in the Italian economy for farm tractors. Revitalization of the farm economy required tractors, but parts and equipment were very scarce. Lamborghini proceeded to piece together simple but effective tractors from whatever military surplus he could gather. Soon, he was designing and building tractors from the ground up. Within five years after the war, he was able to build his first modern factory. Success continued and he became a wealthy industrialist within 10 years.

To fulfill his passion for fast cars, Lamborghini had purchased a number of Ferraris.   He enjoyed tuning them to his own specifications to get yet more power. He drove hard and fast, but eventually became disenchanted with what he felt was a weak point in the Ferrari clutch. Much has been made of Lamborghini's visit to the Ferrari factory to express his concern to Enzo Ferrari directly. He suggested that since he was building strong clutch units for his tractors, perhaps he could design a new heavy-duty clutch for Ferrari. Ferrari, not impressed, is reported to have said, "Lamborghini, you build tractors, and I'll build sports cars." Rebuffed by Ferrari, Lamborghini decided that he would cure that problem, along with some other Ferrari deficiencies, by building his own sports car.

He started the automotive design work in a section of his tractor factory at nearby Cento. Lamborghini needed a building dedicated solely to the new sports car venture. In 1963, he built a striking new factory in St. Agata, located just 15 miles from Ferrari's factory near Maranello. Lamborghini proceeded on a distinctive course, hiring some very creative engineers, young but experienced. Giotto Bizzarrini was commissioned to design a new V-12 engine. Giampaolo Dallara and Paolo Stanzani headed the chassis and body design team, and New Zealander Bob Wallace was the test 'pilota'.

It's interesting to reflect on what ultimately became of this young engineering staff. Dallara is now a Formula I chassis designer and constructor. Bizzarrini gained fame with the Strada and other sports cars bearing his name. Stanzani was recently the technical director of the reborn Bugatti firm in France. Wallace has had his own mechanical restoration shop in Phoenix for nearly 20 years.

After many models and early successes, when the energy crisis occurred in the early 1970s, Lamborghini made a personal decision to step out of the car manufacturing business and into a retirement of sorts. When Bolivia canceled a large tractor order, the combined enterprises faced a financial crisis, as Lamborghini had been investing tractor profits in his sports car company. Having recently invested heavily in new factory equipment and the design of his upcoming Urraco model, he found himself strapped for cash. He sold the tractor company to Same Trattori SpA, a rival tractor manufacturer, and he sold 51% of the car company to a Swiss businessman named Rossetti. Two years later in 1974, he sold the remaining 49% to another Swiss, Rene Leimer.

Lamborghini relocated to Lake Trasimeno in central Italy, near Perugia. Here he entered a new business venture-winemaking. Acquiring a large tract of land, he planted vineyards. Running true to form, he invested heavily in the latest state-of-the-art manufacturing and bottling machinery for his wine business. The winery continues very successfully today. Most of its product is exported from Italy, but not to the US.

Sig. Lamborghini remains very active today, tilling the soil in La Fiorita's vineyards on one of his tractors or putting in a full physical work day in the factory or shops. He has assembled a small museum and keeps a selection of models of the early cars and tractors. He is presently converting part of La Fiorita into a vacation resort with apartments, tennis courts and a golf course. Golf courses need golf carts, and Lamborghini is now at work designing his own, which, like everything else he produces, will likely be innovative. Considering that his world-wide fame rests on fewer than 7,000 sports cars to date that bear the raging bull emblem, Ferruccio Lamborghini is a rarity among the rare.

THE LAMBORGHINI V-12 ENGINE

The Lamborghini V-12 engine deserves special mention. It is one of few V-12 designs that was near perfect at its inception and has stood the test of time for over a quarter of a century. Bizzarrini's most recent prior fame had resulted from his engineering design of the Ferrari 250 GTO race car. Commissioned by Ferruccio Lamborghini to design a 3.5-liter engine for his new sportscar venture, Bizzarrini was virtually given a free hand. Bizzarrini based his design on a 1.5-liter Formula I racing engine he had penned in the past, but couldn't get Enzo Ferrari to authorize while he was working there.

Bizzarrini came up with an aluminum-alloy-block V-12 with alloy heads. Its four overhead camshafts were chain driven. Most of Lamborghini's competitors at that time were still using single-overhead camshafts. This 3.5-liter V-12 breathed through six two-barrel Weber downdraft carburetors. It had twin Marelli distributors, driven off the camshafts on each side of the engine. It produced 360-370 bhp on the dynamometer at 8,000 rpm.

Ferruccio Lamborghini thought this was a bit too racy an engine for his intended use. He wanted a very smooth, refined V-12, capable of lasting 45,000 miles before any major work was necessary. Bizzarrini was not interested in detuning his very healthy design, as that would compromise his desire to build an all-out competition engine.

So Lamborghini had chassis engineer Gianpaolo Dallara perform the detuning of Bizzarrini's design in 1964. Downdraft carburetors were replaced with six side-draft 40DCOE Webers, which allowed future body designs to have a low hood. The racing-derived dry-sump lubrication was replaced by a more conventional wet-sump system. Milder camshaft grinds reduced power to 320 bhp at 7,000 rpm. In this form, Lamborghini had the powerful, but dependable and tractable (remember, this is a tractor manufacturer) V-12 engine he was looking for.

This revised V-12 engine went into production for the 1964 350GT, and remained virtually unchanged throughout the 400GT 2+2, Islero, Espada, Jarama, and 1974-85 Countach. The only basic change was increasing the capacity from 3.5 to 4.0 to 4.7 liters during this 22-year period of use. These V-12 engines remained virtually indestructible throughout this time in spite of the displacement and horsepower increases.

Problems rarely occur with the crankshaft, rods, pistons, engine block, or cylinder heads. The bottom end is good for 100,000 miles if properly cared for. The top end of this radical four-overhead-camshaft V-12 has a 40,000+ mile range. Overhaul encompasses chain replacement, valve grind and adjustment, and possibly distributor bearing replacement due to the horizontal placement of the Marelli dual-point distributors. All Lamborghini V-12 engines were mated to 5-speed transmissions.

THE LAMBORGHINI GT CARS

350GTV

The very first Lamborghini was built by Carrozzeria Sargiotto of Turin and shown at the 1963 Turin Auto Show. This was a 2-place, aluminum bodied car designed by Franco Scaglione. The 3.5-liter V-12 motor was the original 370 bhp Bizzarrini design. It was trailed by a 5-speed ZF transmission and Salisbury rear differential. The engine and drive train received accolades from the motoring press, but the body design was not well-received by the press nor by Sig. Lamborghini himself. After languishing at the factory for most of its life, the show car was restored in 1989 and resides at Emilianauto, a Bologna Lamborghini dealer.

350GT

Lamborghini 350 GT   *Jim Kaminski Photo*

The first actual production model appeared at the 1964 Geneva Auto Show. The aforementioned GTV was redesigned by

Carrozzeria Touring of Milan into a much softer design, with more cohesive, flowing lines. Coachwork was aluminum panels wrapped around a steel tube framework, a "superleggera" process patented by Touring. The 3.5-liter V-12 was detuned to 320 bhp. A 5-speed ZF transmission was connected to the Salisbury differential. Independent suspension was used at all four corners, a relative rarity on sports cars of the period. Borrani wire wheels were standard. Most 350GTs had Girling brake systems and Koni shock absorbers all around. Top speed was about 150 mph, and it was considered to be the smoothest running Gran Turismo sports car of its time. Approximately 120 cars were completed during 1964-1966, including two 350GTS spyder versions. There are no weak points in either the drive train or coachwork. Current values should be $85,000-$150,000, with mint examples even higher.

400GT (Interim)

Early in 1965, the factory finished a V-12 updated from 3.5 to 4.0 liters, which was first shown at the New York Auto Show in April. An increase in the bore was the only change performed. This engine was intended for use in an upcoming 2+2 version of the 350GT. Meanwhile, customers could order either the 3.5 or 4.0-liter engine in a two-seat 350GT style body. Supposedly only 23 of these "400GT Interim" cars were produced for customers who chose the 4.0-liter version engine. Virtually all were clothed in steel panels, but kept the 350GT style body shape. Lamborghini also developed its proprietary 5-speed transmission and rear differential at this time. The new transmission built in-house was found to be quieter than the ZF used in the 350GT. Most 400GT Interim cars had these new parts in the drive train. Virtually the entire drive train was now manufactured within the Lamborghini factory. Today's values range from $90,000 to $150,000.

400GT 2+2

In 1966, the factory released a new car with 2+2 seating at the Geneva Motor Show. The body shell was identical to the 350GT, but it now had two bucket seats squeezed into the area behind the driver. This space had been a luggage rack in the 350GT, and the rear seats protruded five inches farther into the trunk area. Overall body length remained the same on the 350GT and the 400GT 2+2. Virtually the only distinguishable exterior difference was that the 400GT 2+2 rear window was five inches shorter than the prior 350GT. Single oval Hella headlamps in the 350GT were replaced by dual round headlamps on each side of the 400GT 2+2 and the 400GT Interim.

The newly developed 4.0-liter version of the V-12 was used exclusively in the new 2+2. The 2+2 had a single fuel filler on the right rear, while the 350GT had fillers on both sides. While the 350GT sat parallel to the ground, the new 400GT 2+2 was slightly raised in the rear due to suspension changes to compensate for the extra weight of rear passengers, if and when any might be aboard. Reportedly, 247 of the 400GT 2+2 were finished during 1966-1968. Performance was very similar to the 350GT. Two 400GT 2+2 chassis were rebodied by outside carrozzerie into the Monza 400 and the Flying Star. Prices of the 400GT 2+2 presently range between $75,000 to $140,000.

Islero

Built from 1968, the Islero was basically a 400GT 2+2 clothed in a new body style. It retained the same frame and suspension as the 400GT 2+2, but had much stiffer anti-roll bars front and rear. The drive train was identical to the 400GT 2+2. It stands about one inch taller than the 400GT 2+2. Most Isleros were fitted with the Miura-style Campagnolo wheels. Body panels were steel, similar to the 400GT 2+2. The Islero was quite a bit faster than the 400GT 2+2, especially on the lower end of the speed scale. This model initially suffered lean sales, as Lamborghini admirers were not stimulated by its sober, non-extravagant design. It has found many ardent followers though in recent years. Lamborghini completed 125 in 1968, before updating the model with the Islero S. Prices range from $65,000 to $130,000.

Lamborghini Islero   *Jim Kaminski Photo*

Islero S

This car was virtually the same as the preceding Islero. New profile camshafts added 15 bhp. Slight flares were added to the wheel arches. The air scoop in the center of the hood was enlarged and vents were added on the side of the front fenders, just behind the front wheels. The rear suspension was stiffened a bit more. The interior was restyled quite a bit, however. A fan-shaped design was stitched into the seat bottoms. Many Islero Ss had cloth inserts in the center of the seats, while the outside portions remained leather. Production was 100 units in 1969. Values range from $75,000 to $140,000.

Miura P400

This was the first of three series of the innovative Miura. Named after the legendary strain of Spanish fighting bulls from the Don Eduardo Miura ranch, the car uses a transverse-mounted V-12 engine placed amidships. The 41"-tall car had a steel roof and center-section and the tilt-up front and rear body sections were aluminum. From the 125th Miura built, the chassis box sections were increased from 0.9mm to 1.0mm thickness steel for additional strength. The V-12 is the same basic 4-1iter block used in earlier models, but the transmission and differential were cast together as a integral part of the lower end of the engine sump area. During 1966-1969, 374 examples came off the assembly-line.

Also the Miura was the first production car to ever use the horizontal rear window slats, now a common sight on sports and sporty cars of the last 20 years. These features support the fact that the Lamborghini factory was creating many "firsts" in the production sports car industry. The 350 bhp V-12 produced 170+ mph speeds. One of the most beautiful cast (magnesium-aluminum alloy) wheels ever designed was the Campagnolo used first on the Miura and later on some 400GT's, the Islero, Jarama, and Espada series I and II. In the 1960s, factory test drivers from Lamborghini, Ferrari and Maserati would complete high-speed testing on the 105 mile autostrada from Milan to Modena. Lamborghini test driver Bob Wallace once covered the entire distance in a Miura at an average of 161.5 mph. Values range from $80,000-$150,000.

Miura P400 S

In early 1969, the Miura was improved to the "S" version. Air conditioning was added as an option, as were electric windows being made standard. Different camshafts and combustion chambers moved horsepower to 370 bhp and speed to 175 mph. Gussets in chassis corners made the chassis stiffer than on the earlier series. Rear suspension was modified to reduce squat during acceleration. Interiors were upgraded from vinyl to leather in most cases. Vented brake discs replaced solid discs on most of the "S" models. Values range from $100,000 to $175,000 on the 140 Miura Ss built from 1969 to 1971.

Miura P400 SV

Again handling and speed improvements resulted in the 1971-1972

Miura SV. Further strengthening of the chassis continued. Both front and rear suspension were updated for better handling yet. Prior to the SV, the engine and differential shared a common oil sump, hence gear and synchro particles were introduced into the engine oil, endangering bearing life on the crank. Except for the first 50 cars, the SV series enjoyed a newly separated sump, correcting this design deficiency. However, experience shows this not to have been a critical problem. It only reduced the longevity of bearing life by 25% or less. On current Miuras, which rarely have accumulated more than 35,000 miles, it has not destroyed anything in the bottom end. They have merely required earlier rebuilding, but nothing drastic happens to the Miuras with a shared sump. Under constant long-term competition-type use, this feature may have affected the life of a Miura V-12, but few ever have been run hard for long periods of time.

Speed in the SV was increased to 180 mph with awesome acceleration, considering power was now up to 385 bhp. Air conditioning was again an option, but rarely ordered. The SV is physically more imposing due to the widening of the rear bonnet by three inches to accommodate new nine-inch-wide rear Campagnolo alloy wheels. These were equipped with Pirelli 285/60-VR15 tires. Production was 140 cars in 1971-1972. Values range from $250,000-$325,000.

Two one-off Miuras were built in addition to the normal production cars. One open-top roadster was built by Bertone for exhibition purposes and still exists in England. The second was the Jota, which was a rolling test-bed type of vehicle built by test driver/engineer Bob Wallace. It featured a super-light-weight body and chassis, and had a 440 bhp V-12. After being sold to a customer, it crashed and burned in Brescia, Italy in the mid-1970s.

Espada

The Espada series was fathered by the Bertone show car, the Marzal. In 1967, Bertone built a 4-passenger car, with gull-wing doors made nearly entirely of glass. It had a 6-cylinder engine developed by cutting a Miura V-12 in half. It was mounted at the very rear of the car, similar to the Miura. Ferruccio Lamborghini now has the Marzal in his personal collection.

Espada I

The Series I debuted at the Geneva Show in 1968. It was significantly changed from the Marzal show car, but retained the basic shape. It was a full four-passenger, two-door, 150 mph sports car, sitting 46.6" tall. Two adults are very comfortable in the rear seats. It used the same V-12 engine and 5-speed drive train as the Islero. Rating was at 320 bhp, due to the drag in driving the air-conditioning compressor. The body is steel and the engine hood is aluminum. The huge glass rear hatch window raises to allow a vast amount of luggage to be stowed for touring. The Series I is most easily recognized by its octagonal shaped instrument housing directly behind the steering wheel. Miura-style Campagnolo knockoff wheels anchored the Pirelli tires. Air-conditioning was standard, as were electric windows. During 1968-1969, 186 were produced by Lamborghini. Values range from $25,000-$50,000.

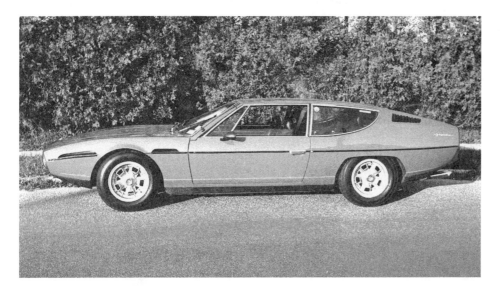

Lamborghini Espada   *Howard Kestenbaum Photo*

Espada II

The Series II arrived in 1970. An increase in compression ratio added power to the V-12, now 350 bhp. Air pumps were added to US cars, but the pump cut out at high revolutions for no loss of power. A drop in the floor pan gave rear passengers an extra 3/4" headroom. The main change was a more standardized dash design, with wood panels surrounding the instrument cluster facing. Some very late Series II cars had a new smooth-faced, 5-bolt Campagnolo wheel, replacing the knockoff wheels. Tailight lenses were changed slightly also. Some 575 units were completed during 1970-1972. Values range from $25,000-$50,000.

Espada III

The third series of Espada, in late 1972, once again was headlined by a change in the dashboard layout. The center of the dash was angled towards the driver. The instrument cluster facing was now brushed aluminum. A leather bound steering wheel replaced the wood-rimmed wheel in the Series I & II. The grillework was changed slightly. The new smooth-faced, bolt-on wheels were standard on the Series III, while only a few of the the Series II cars had this new wheel. Power steering was now an option and almost every car had it. A Chrysler Torqueflite automatic transmission (horrors!) was also an option now.

For US cars, DOT bumpers were added. On the 1973 cars, a large black, plastic pod protruded from each side of the bumper, front and rear. From 1975 to 1978, a full width plastic bumper was installed front and rear. Technically, the full bumper cars were Series IV, but nearly always are referred to as Series III by experts and collectors. No change in performance ratings took place. During 1972-1978, 463 units were produced. Current values are $25,000-$60,000.

Jarama

The Jarama entered the scene early in 1970 at the Geneva Motor

Austin-Healey 100-4 and Bugeye Sprite

Porsche 356A 1500GS Carrera

Courtesy of Leonard Turner

Ferrari 275 GTB/4 Long Nose

MGA

Lamborghini Jarama

Maserati 3500 Vignale Spyder

Jaguar XJ-S Coupe

Courtesy of Jaguar

Mercedes 300 S

Ferrari 250 SWB Berlinetta

Porsche 911 Speedsters

Courtesy of Leonard Turner

BMW 328, M1, 507

Courtesy of Bill Siuru

Maserati Ghibli

Courtesy of Francis Mandarano

Courtesy of Triumph

Triumph TR 3 A

Alfa Romeo 6C 1750

Courtesy of Nicky Wright

Jaguar XK-E Roadster

MG-TF's

Show. Similar in layout to the Espada, it was a four-passenger, two-door design. But it was not as roomy in the rear seats as the Espada. This resulted from the shortest wheelbase, by almost three inches, of any Lamborghini ever built. The drivetrain was the same as the Espada, with the front-mounted V-12 and 5-speed transmission. Power rating was at 350 bhp. It was only 200 pounds lighter than the Espada, even though five inches shorter in wheelbase.

Lamborghini Jarama   *Jeff Dworin Photo*

Jarama was a very nimble, exciting car due to this short wheelbase. Body panels were steel as in the Espada. Steering required some effort at low speeds, due to lack of power-steering. But high-speed handling was very respectable. It still managed 6.8 seconds from 0-60 mph in 1970, keeping up with most of the muscle cars of the period. Some late 1972 models had two rectangular lift-off roof panels directly over the driver and passenger. Wheels were the Miura-style Campagnolo. The most recognizable features of the Jarama are the headlight covers, which when down cover only half the headlights, blending in with the sheet metal of the nose which wraps over the face of the car. There were 177 of these cars produced and they have values of $25,000-$70,000.

Jarama S

The first Jarama series was produced from 1970-1972. In 1972, it was improved into the "S" version. Power was upgraded to 365 bhp partially due to a more efficient exhaust system. A large air scoop was added to the engine hood. Air vents were added to the sides of the front fenders, just behind the wheels. (Some late series I Jarama's also had these vents.) A major change in the dashboard layout also occurred. Bumpers had a very slight change. Standard wheels changed to the bolt-on, smooth-faced Campagnolos. Production from 1972-1976 was 150 units. Values are $30,000-$90,000.

Urraco P250

Built from 1971-1975, Urraco carried the first Lamborghini V-8 engine. A 2.5-liter, single-overhead-camshaft engine, this unit delivered 220 bhp at 7500 rpm. Four Weber two-barrel carburetors fueled the engine. Again, as in the V-12, the block and heads were of aluminum. The body was called a 2+2, but the rear seats did not include any perceptible leg room in front of them. Body panels were steel, with unibody construction as in the Espada and Jarama. MacPherson strut suspension was employed at all four corners, certainly a first on a high-performance sports car. The body design by Bertone was a neat, compact breath of brilliance. The short wheelbase and body, plus rack and pinion steering provided a superbly handling car. The handling gives a driver the feel of a go-cart, as it is very quick and exhilarating. Production was 522 units. Values range from $20,000-$40,000.

Urraco P200

This version was built in 1975 and 1976 for the Italian market, which had heavy taxes levied on cars above 2 liters. The engine was downsized internally to 2 liters with 182 bhp. Production was 68 cars. Values range from $20,000- $30,000. These are (fortunately) rarely found outside of Europe.

Urraco P300

This iteration was produced from 1975-1979. The engine was changed immensely, and for the better. Twin camshafts were placed on both banks, driven by chains instead of the belt drive of the P250. Internal size was increased to 3 liters and new heads were developed. This yielded 250 bhp, making the P300 performance quite a bit superior to the P250. Engine reliability improved also. Tests seem to validate almost 160 mph now. Most P300 cars are recognizable by the black plastic DOT bumpers front and rear. However, late 250's also had the new DOT body style.

The slats placed horizontally over the rear window on all Urracos marked the continuation of this feature, which had been introduced first on the 1966 Miura. Some French Urracos replaced the slats with a flat engine cover, due to French visibility regulations. Total production of the P300 was 205 units. Values range from $25,000-$55,000.

Lamborghini Silhouette   *Albert Romavari Photo*

Silhouette

The car marked the next evolution from the Urraco. Built from 1976-1978, its drive train was the same as the P300 Urraco. Suspension was revamped, with 285/40-VR15 Pirelli P7s added. Wide rear fender flares housed the muscular rear end of the car. The side rear window of the P300 Urraco was deleted, a wider pillar installed, and a removable top incorporated. This resulted in a targa-top styling. Flares were also added to the front wheel openings. Rounded wheel openings changed to a squared-off look. The rear window slats of the P300 were removed, and a tunnel styling was placed over the rear mounted V-8. Only 54 of the Silhouette models were completed. Values range from $40,000 - $90,000.

Jalpa

Again, the next new model was an evolutionary change from the Silhouette. Built from 1982-1988, its engine displacement was increased to 3.5 liters, to increase horsepower to 255 bhp. Lower profile P7 Pirellis were now on 16" wheels. Sheetmetal on the nose was softened somewhat from the Silhouette. A smooth-faced, more subdued wheel was added. However, in 1988 the Silhouette-style wheel with the 5 large round ports was again being offered on the Jalpa. As in all the Urracos and the Silhouette, the Jalpa body panels were in steel. Production was 410 examples. Values range from $30,000-$60,000.

LM002

A descendant of the ill-fated Cheetah designed in 1977 (which never reached production), this is unquestionably the wildest off-road vehicle in the world. Produced from 1985 to today, the LM002 stands six feet tall, weighs 5,990 pounds, and is even wider than a Countach. It is powered by the Countach 5.2-liter, 425 bhp, four-valve V-12. driving a 5-speed transmission with all-wheel drive. In safari trim, it features full four-passenger luxury interior with air-conditioning. It has almost 12" of ground clearance. Pirelli developed special tires for sand usage, and they are 325/65VR-17s that cost over $1,000.00 each. Body is of aluminum and fiberglass. Performance is 8.5 seconds from 0-60 mph and 126 mph top speed. It handles like a sports car and is remarkably easy to drive. The tires make very little road noise. Production to present is approximately 350 units. Values are $70,000-$160,000.

Countach

To many, especially those relatively new to automotive exotica, the name Lamborghini cannot be spoken apart from Countach. The name is derived from a slang remark from the area around Turin, Italy. It is an exclamation of amazement, roughly translating to 'Wow!.' Correct Italian pronunciation is "KOON-tatch", with the last syllable sounding like "watch". However, most English speaking countries pronounce it "KOON tash". I even hear Italians say it the English way now, and this seems to be the majority pronunciation.

Countach LP500

The prototype of this two-decade-old phenomenon was introduced in 1971 at the Geneva Motor Show and destroyed by the factory during DOT crash testing in England in 1973.

Countach LP400

The first production model carried the lower model number, and some 150 examples were produced from 1974 to 1977. The design featured aluminum body panels over a tubular frame. This first series did not have the rear wing nor the fender flares so commonly seen today. It was 400-500 pounds lighter by most reports than later series of Countaches. Earlier cars had magnesium hubs. Approximately the first ten to twelve cars had periscope rear-view mirrors built into the roof. Later cars had outside fender mirrors. Wheels were 9 1/2" wide and mounted with 215/70VR-14 Michelin XWX tires. Wheel rims were nearly identical to the Urraco wheel.

The engine block internals remained the same design and 4.0-liter size as the past V-12s used for 15 years. The engine produced 375 bhp at 8,000 rpm. The V-12 was mounted longitudinally just in front of the rear axle. The front of the engine was facing to the rear and the transmission was towards the front of the car in a normal position between the seats. The driveshaft ran through the bottom of the sump area, connecting with the driveshafts at the very rearward portion of the car. Top speed was 180+ mph. Values range from $80,000-$150,000.

Countach LP400S

There were 237 of these cars produced from 1978 to 1982. The suspension was entirely re-engineered, both front and rear. This was to allow space for an entirely new Pirelli tire developed specifically for the Countach, the ultra-wide P7. The rear was shod with 305/35VR-15, changing from the 14" wheels of the LP400. Brakes were changed from Girling to ATE units, with larger calipers to handle the larger tires. A chin spoiler was added under the nose. Wide flares were added to house the new P7 Pirellis. A new wheel with 5 oval holes was added, and we still see it on the majority of Countaches today. A rear wing was optional, and a large majority of the cars had it installed. Speed actually was decreased a bit from the preceding model due to the drag from the wing and wide tires. Prices today range from $90,000-$120,000.

Countach 5000S

During 1982-1985, Lamborghini produced 323 of this updated model. The engine capacity was increased to 4.7 liters, but it is basically called a 5-1iter by most enthusiasts. The engine block was beefed up internally. Compression was lowered from 10.5:1 to 9.2:1 for better burning of the low octane fuel becoming commonplace. Horsepower was still at 375 bhp, producing speeds of 180 mph. A portion of these had the floorpan lowered, giving 3/4" extra in headroom. Values range from $95,000-$120,000.

Countach 5000S Quattrovalve

In the period 1985-1988, 610 of the new 'Quattrovalve' were completed. Capacity increased to 5.2 liters. Four-valve cylinder heads were created and the block again restructured for additional stiffness. The Quattrovalve now became a high-tech engine, very close to racing specifications and design. Compression moved up to 9.5:1 and horsepower to 425 bhp on US cars. DOT standards were met for the US with the addition of bumpers added at the factory. Two black pods pointed skyward on each side of the front bumper, to conform with bumper-height regulations. In the rear, four individual black pods, spaced across the tail, housed the DOT shock absorber mechanisms. These were unsightly in most people's opinions, but necessary for the short-sighted Department of Transportation. The first 10 or so 1985s came into the US with downdraft Weber carburetors lined-up down the center of the engine, but thereafter US cars came with fuel-injection from the factory. In 1988, side skirts with air intakes were added to the rocker panel area of the bodywork. Some late 1988s were called 88 1/2 when a new climate-control air-conditioning system was added. Values range from $100,000-$130,000.

Countach Anniversary

To celebrate the 25th anniversary of the Lamborghini, 700 examples of this restyled Countach were produced in 1989 and 1990. The last Countach came off the assembly line July 4, 1990. Openings in the radiator ducts and engine bay ducts were now running the length of the car, instead of the previous ductwork perpendicular to the length of the car. Integrated bumpers now flowed into the basic lines of the car. A new modular wheel from OZ in Italy was mounted with the Pirellis. The bucket seats were entirely redesigned, as was much of the interior. Drag on the body was reduced, resulting in a speed increase to 186 mph. Values now range from $160,000 to $200,000.

Diablo

Making its debut in August 1990, the Diablo didn't reach the US until about April, 1991. A large hint of the Countach remains, but it's actually an entirely new design. The upswinging doors of the Countach remain. A new side window design slopes downward at an angle just behind the rear wheel. The totally new body design gives a 0.31 Cd compared to the brick-like 0.40 Cd of the Countach. Already the Diablo has been timed at 204 mph with electronic timers in Italy, and this is a US-legal car. The V-12 was upsized to 5.7 liters, with major changes to the interiors, and with fuel-injection produces 492 bhp. Sticker price is $240,000 and approximately 150 have been built to date. This new raging bull has proved that it is the fastest production sportscar in the world today.

CLUBS

Lamborghini Owners Club
PO Box 7214
St. Petersburg, FL 33734

Lamborghini Club of America
170 Monte Vista Road
Orinda, CA 94563

ABOUT THE AUTHOR

Jim Kaminski of St. Petersburg, Florida is president of the Lamborghini Owners' Club, having founded it in 1978. It is the oldest Lamborghini club in the world, with members in 14 countries. The club is a major source for finding parts, obtaining technical information, appraisals, etc. Kaminski purchased his first Lamborghini in 1973, a 400GT he still has. Ownership of six other Lamborghinis over the years has provided valuable hands-on experience.

YEAR	LINE	Relative Condition: Worse ↔ Better		
		❸	❷	❶
1964—1966	350 GT Coupe	110000	145000	170000
1966—1968	400 GT Coupe	85000	115000	130000
1967—1969	Miura P400 Coupe	145000	160000	180000
1969—1971	Miura P400S Coupe	160000	185000	205000
1971—1972	Miura P400SV Coupe	240000	275000	305000
1968—1969	Islero Coupe	52000	65000	80000
1969	Islero S Coupe	70000	90000	105000
1968—1973	Espada I/II Coupe	30000	38000	45000
1973—1978	Espada III Coupe	34000	40000	48000
1970—1973	Jarama Coupe	40000	50000	65000
1973—1976	Jarama S Coupe	55000	70000	90000
1972—1977	Urraco P250 Coupe	25000	35000	42000
1975—1979	Urraco P300 Coupe	30000	41000	48000
1974—1977	Countach LP400 Coupe	12500	15000	17000
1978—1982	Countach LP400S Coupe	95000	115000	125000
1982—1985	Countach LP500S	90000	105000	120000
1985—1988	Countach LP5000QV Coupe	100000	120000	135000
1989	Countach Anniv. Coupe	180000	185000	195000
1982—1988	Jalpa Coupe	39000	43000	51000

MASERATI

BY FRANCIS MANDARANO

A SHORT COMPANY HISTORY

Since the founding of Officine Alfieri Maserati on December 14, 1914, this small automotive manufacturer changed ownership and control only three times in its first 70 years.

The seven Maserati brothers were born in a small house on the outskirts of Voghera, in the province of Pavia, south of Milano. Their father, Rodolfo, a railroad engineer, married Carolina Losi and moved from Piacanza to Voghera, where they brought up their family of six sons. First was Carlo, born in 1881, then Bindo in 1883, followed by the first Alfieri in 1885, who died during birth. The same name was given to the next son in line, born in 1887. Mario was born in 1890, Ettore in 1894, and lastly, Ernesto in 1898.

In 1903, Carlo went to work for Isotta Fraschini at the age of 22 as a tech advisor and a test driver. Carlo gained quite a reputation there, however, he died in 1919 at the age of 38. Thanks to Carlo, Alfieri was also hired at the age of 18 by Isotta Fraschini, where he made a name for himself as a technician and a test driver. He was later followed by his younger brothers, Bindo and Ettore.

In 1914, Alfieri organized his own company, along with five mechanics and his two younger brothers, 20-year-old Ettore and 16-year-old Ernesto. Alfieri started making race modifications to Isotta Fraschini mechanics, and the demand was strong. Like a modern-day Reeves Callaway or AMG, Alfieri prepared cars and won races of the period with his specially-tuned Isottas.

In 1925, Alfieri made the commitment to build a complete car carrying the name Maserati. The company's "Trident" logo came from Neptune's spear, taken from the statue in the center of Bologna. Alfieri Maserati ran his company until March 3, 1932, when, at the early age of 44, he died during an operation on his surviving kidney. The death of Alfieri Maserati was a great setback for the company, and a loss to the people of Bologna, who considered him one of their own. The town fell out in mass to mourn their fallen hero.

Bindo then left Isotta Franschini where he'd worked for more than 20 years, and together with his brothers Ettore and Ernesto picked up the remaining pieces of the family company. The three moved ahead in the great tradition of Alfieri, and continued his unfinished work in a way that would have made him proud. For five years, the company built racing cars and sold them to sportsmen of the day.

Then, in 1937, the brothers decided to sell the majority shares to a wealthy Modenese family of industrialists, the Orsis. Adolfo Orsi, the founder, had built a conglomerate that owned interests in such industries as steel manufacturing, agricultural machinery, tool manufacturing, and public transportation (including the local trolley line). What interested the Orsis most was Maserati's spark plug manufacturing business and not so much the automobile division. They saw the potential in the work force to produce other products. As it turned out, the race cars helped them penetrate the Argentine market with their machine tools and other products.

Omar Orsi, Adolfo's son, was assigned to manage the newly acquired Maserati works. At first Omar's management style was very discreet. But, as time passed, he gradually took more control, and the Maserati brothers were slowly moved into non-management positions. The brothers stayed on under a 10-year engineering and design contract that expired in 1947. Then, they left Modena, and went back home to Bologna to start a new company building racing cars under the name of Officine Specializzate Construsione Automobili, which we know by the acronym OSCA.

The Orsis continued to operate the Maserati Factory for another 30 years, overseeing the change from building and competing racing cars to making powerful GT cars. Maserati continued to introduce new models until 1968, when the majority of the company shares changed hands once again - this time to Citroen. But the French connection didn't last, and seven years later circumstances forced Citroen to issue a statement that officially put the Maserati company into liquidation to be sold to the highest bidder.

On August 8, 1975, with the Italian government as his partner, Alejandro DeTomaso, the 47-year-old Argentine ex-race car driver and founder of the car company bearing his own name, became the fourth owner of Maserati. Having raced 2-liter Maseratis and OSCA cars, DeTomaso became an enthusiastic and sympathetic owner of the company.

In the early 1980s, Chrysler Chairman Lee Iaccoca agreed with Sig. DeTomaso to purchase 16% of Maserati's stock (which Chrysler still owned as of July, 1991). The agreement called for Maserati to manufacture a car for Chrysler known as the TC, the Turbo Coupe. Approximately 6,000 cars were produced before the agreement ended abruptly, with Chrysler losing millions. In the turmoil, Chrysler bought Lamborghini. Note: The TC was a giant flop on the market, however, it is a car of very high quality and deserves consideration.

Then in 1990, with Maserati's Biturbo sales slumping, Sig. DeTomaso acquired yet another partner. This time Fiat purchased 49% of the firm with options to purchase the balance. On August 8, 1991, DeTomaso celebrated 16 years at the helm of Maserati. The word is out, however, that he is seeking to step down and retire.

THE EARLY RACING CARS

In the 1920s, Maserati made winning race cars, like the Tipo 26 and 26B, 26MM (for Mille Miglia). In the 1930s, the world saw winning sport and racing cars such as the Tipo 8C 2800, Tipo 8CM and the great pre-war race car, Tipo 4CL. Maserati won the Indianapolis 500 in 1939 and 1940 with Wilbur Shaw at the wheel of the powerful 8CTF. Pre-war cars are very collectible with prices ranging from $600,000 to $1,000,000 or more for a car with a good history. These cars are usually owned by motoring museums or large collections, and seldom become available.

After the war, Maserati produced such great racing cars as the beautiful A6GCS, 300S, 450S, and the car Fangio drove to his fifth world championship at the Nurburgring in 1957, the much sought-after and highly-coveted 250F Formula I car, to name just a few. These models are rare and highly collectible, with 1991 prices ranging from $700,000 to $1.5 million.

A6G Series GT Cars

In the late 1940s and early 1950s, Maserati produced a limited run of GT cars known as the A6G series. Perhaps no more than 140 A6GCS cars were made over a seven-year period. The early A6Gs had single-cam, 6-cylinder engines, and a definite sporty flair and feel. During this period the Italian coach building industry, centered in and around Torino, was blossoming and gaining world-wide recognition for producing gorgeous body styling.

For their road cars, Maserati always used outside designers, including such famous names as Pininfarina, Bertone, Zagato, Frua, Allemano, Vignale and Touring. Maserati, therefore, produced some very beautiful and collectible cars. The evolution of the A6G series in the mid-1950s included the addition of dual overhead cams, twin ignition and triple Weber side-draft carburetors, all of which substantially increased the horsepower.

A few highly-collectible A6G series cars left the factory equipped with the A6GCS racing engine, with gear cam drive instead of chains, and dual distributors. Early A6G cars in excellent condition can fetch $150,000 or more, with some special models like spyders and Zagato-bodied cars bringing three or more times as much. Some racing versions with a good history could pass the million dollar mark.

But alas, the company's overhead was too much and their income not enough. The racing department was spending an enormous amount of money on research and development to introduce new models to meet the ever-changing racing rules. The coup de grace came at Caracas, Venezuela, in 1958 when five factory team cars were crashed in competition. Simultaneously, Argentina defaulted on payments to Maserati for purchased machine tools. The decision was made to quit racing altogether.

The Orsis decided to concentrate on a new GT car that could be produced in mass quantities, by Italian standards at least, and sold to the sporting enthusiasts of the day. They felt this would solve their financial problems.

The 3500 GT

The 3500 GT was introduced to the motoring world at the 1957 Geneva Auto Show. The factory geared up to produce a whopping five cars a day. By the time 1965 had rolled around, they had produced almost 2,000 of the 3500 GT cars. Using the experience they gained from many years of racing, the factory equipped the 3500 GT with an all-aluminum in-line six that was derived from the 350S racing engine, and featured twin ignition, dual overhead cams, triple Weber carburetors, etc.

The coachwork was by Touring of Milan and was executed in all aluminum, therefore, the name "superleggera," meaning super light. The 3500 had a long nose, the classic Maserati oval grille, and was fitted with a luxurious English Connolly leather interior, a ZF transmission from Germany and the top-of-the-line Girling brakes of the period. It was available in such colors as foam green, black, white, navy blue, silver, and of course, red. (One trademark of Maserati is that its cars are not always red like 95% of all Ferraris.) The 3500GT quickly gained market acceptance.

The 3500 was for the sportsman who required luxury and power, not merely light weight and top speed. The first series 3500 GT was followed up by the second series car, designated 3500 GTi. It now carried Lucas fuel injection and other subtle refinements and body changes. A spyder version was produced by Vignale on a shorter chassis. (Later, Vignale was also commissioned to produce a model called the Sebring on that same shortened chassis.)

Early Production 3500 GT Features

Weber carburetors
Drum brakes on rear and disc on front
Smaller type water pump
Borrani steel wheels with script
Most fitted with 4-speed transmission
Non-reclining seats
Under dash emergency brake
Front vent window per door
Crank up windows
Aluminum body

Late production 3500 GTI Features

Lucas fuel injection
4-wheel Girling disc brakes
Larger water pump with magnetic fan
More cars fitted with 16" wheels
5-speed ZF S5-17 transmission
Upgraded bucket seat with reclining mechanism
Floor-mounted pull-up type emergency brake
Two vent windows per door
Aluminum body
Larger windshield

3500 Vignale Spyder

A spyder version of the 3500 GT, produced by Alfredo Vignale from a design of Michelotti, his in-house designer, these cars are an absolute dream to drive. They're very sporty, with good road manners, an easy-to-operate top, and lots of room in the trunk (and in the boot area with the top up). Of all the 3500 GTs, including the first and second series Touring cars, certainly the Vignale spyders are the most collectible. Most people agree that approximately 245 were built, making the appreciation potential excellent. The Vignale spyder is definitely a car that you could drive on a daily basis. Expect to see prices from $125,000-$145,000 for a superb car.

Sebring

The Sebring was Maserati's first car to begin the tradition of 2+2 cars being named for race tracks where Maserati enjoyed success, such as the win at Sebring on March 23, 1957. Fangio and Behra co-drove the 450S factory team car, leading the entire race, and setting new track records. Other 2+2 cars would follow with names from such tracks as Mexico, Indy, Kyalami, etc. The Sebring was introduced as an up-market 3500 GTi with swoopier lines designed by Alfredo Vignale; its rakish styling caught on quickly. The four-headlight frontal area distinguishes it from the Touring-bodied car of the same period.

Maserati Sebring   *MIE Archive Photo*

Sebrings were equipped with the same fuel-injected, in-line six-cylinder engine fitted to the 3500 GTi. The later version was enlarged to four liters and equipped with 15" Borrani wire wheels and Pirelli tires, transforming it into a superb high-speed, great-handling GT car. Good to very nice examples are available in the $35-45,000 range and exceptional examples reach the $45-55,000 range.

First series Sebring

3.5-liter in-line six-cylinder engine
Lucas fuel injection
Jaeger gauges
Round style 3500 GT tail lights
16" Borrani steel disk wheels with logo hub caps
Many cars equipped with 16" wire wheels
Five-speed ZF S5-17 transmission
No air conditioning
Early style oil cooler with external oil pump
Early style oil filter canister

Second Series Sebring

3.7 and 4-liter in-line six-cylinder engine
Lucas fuel injection
Late style dash
Smith gauges
Mexico/Quattroporte I-type tail lights
15" Borrani wire wheels available as an option
Electric window switches mounted in console
5-speed ZF S5-20 heavy duty aluminum transmission
Air conditioning available as an option
Heat exchanger type oil cooler/warmer

Mistral

In 1963, the 3500 was re-designed again, this time by Frua, and introduced as the Mistral coupe. First shown at the 1963 Turin

Auto Show, the Mistral was a very handsome design, incorporating one of industry's first fast-back designs with a rear hatch that lifts up. That feature became extremely popular in the '70s and '80s. The Mistral was produced in first and second series over a seven-year period, ending in 1970, and came equipped as follows:

Mistral First Series

3.5-liter DOHC six-cylinder engine
ZF S5-17 five-speed transmission
16" Borrani wheels
No center console
Crank-up windows
Jaeger instruments
Battery behind passenger seat
Large black plastic steering wheel

Mistral Second Series

3.7 and 4-liter engines
ZF S5-20 heavy-duty five-speed transmission
15" Borrani wheels
Center console with ash tray
Power windows
Air conditioning a common option
Smaller wood steering wheel
Smith instruments
Battery located in trunk

The Mistral makes a great entry-level Maserati, as it is well balanced with excellent road manners. It's equipped with a superb in-line-six that Maserati has been perfecting since the days of the A6GCS. Sure, the fuel injection can be tempermental, but when set up properly the Lucas injection system will produce great results. An excellent 29-page, simple language, fuel injection tech manual is available from the Maserati Club International (fax them at 206-646-5458); it is an English translation of the best Italian fuel injection tech manual available, with excellent illustrations.

However, if you long for simplicity, the injected engine can be easily converted back to the original Weber carburetor set up with a conversion kit also available from the club.

A number of the coupes were equipped with alloy bodies that make them all a little more collectible. Some had automatic transmissions that were very undesirable. Figure on a cost of $8-10,000 to convert an automatic to a five-speed, so an automatic-equipped car should be discounted accordingly. Prices range from $35-45,000 for excellent examples in today's market.

Maserati Mistral Spyder   Francis Mandarano Photo

Although the Mistral coupe is a great car, the spyder version is the car to collect, as only about 125 examples were made. Very handsome and stylish, it generates a lot of appeal with its Borrani knock-off wire wheels, Connolly leather upholstery, and easy-to-operate top. Later cars have air conditioning that really works. With the top down, the exhaust note is irresistible to the enthusiast's ear. Prices range from $120-150,000 for an excellent car.

THE V-8-ENGINED CARS

5000 GT

The first V-8 GT car to be offered by Maserati was developed in the early part of 1959 and was shown at the Turin Auto Show of that year. The body was by Touring of Milan and was developed on commission for the Shah of Iran, and ever since has been referred to as the Shah's 5000 GT. These cars were built on special order only, with all 32 cars being pre-sold prior to production. They sold for approximately $15-17,000 from 1959 to 1964; this was approximately five times what a Corvette was selling for during the same period, and roughly double the price of its little brother, the 3500 GT.

They were monsters in all respects. The first two cars were equipped with no less than the actual 450S racing engines left over from the racing program that had been killed after the Caracas fiasco. Subsequent 5000 GTs were fitted with an all-new, four-overhead-cam, chain driven V-8 that would later be de-tuned for use in all V-8-equipped Maseratis. Fitted with Lucas fuel injection, dual distributors, and twin plugs per cylinder, it could produce 340-350 HP at 6,000 rpm. Capable of well over 150 mph, these cars had tremendous brute straight line performance. However, on the several occasions I've test driven the 5000, I found the suspension to be inadequate, with an unacceptable amount of sway, and not as well balanced as the in-line six-cylinder cars. The steering is very heavy, but the sound this monster produces is true music to an enthusiast's ears.

"Collectible" is an understatement for the 5000 GT. Of the 32 5000 GTs produced, 16 of them were bodied by Allemano, the balance being built by various coach builders including Pininfarina, Monterosa, Michelotti, Ghia, Frua, Touring and one Bertone car that was actually penned by Giugiaro while he worked there. Luxurious for sure, each car was hand-fitted in Connolly leather to its owner's taste and, because they were all built to special order, no two cars are alike, each one custom-crafted in its own special way. For a nice car in today's market, expect to pay $175,000 to $225,000, down from a high of $350,000 in the fourth quarter of 1989. When purchasing, be sure to get a completely original car. It's better to spend a little more money up front to get the very nicest example you can find, as restoration costs run twice what a normal 3500 GT would require. Parts availability is extremely limited, therefore, anything missing would almost certainly have to be reproduced by hand.

Quattroporte I By Frua

First shown at the 1963 Turin Auto Show along-side the Mistral, the Quattroporte I was a classy, but understated, four-door sedan. Road and Track called it the most luxurious four-door in the world, and they were not wrong.

Early cars were equipped with the 4.2-liter V-8 engine. De-tuned now from the 5000 GT, it was equipped with single ignition, four 38DCNL5 Weber carburetors and four chain-driven overhead camshafts. Very smooth, very quiet, its power was transmitted through a ZF five-speed transmission to a De Dion independent rear suspension. Second Series Quattroportes differed only in that they were fitted with both 4.2 and 4.7-liter engines and with a live axle, and were offered with the optional (but undesirable for the enthusiast) Borg Warner three-speed automatic.

Fun to drive? Very much so. Collectible? Probably not, although at the low prices at which they are being offered, they represent true value and a certain amount of fun. The nicest one in the world would probably fetch no more than $20,000, with most examples in the $9,000 to $12,000 range. The Quattroporte I is probably an excellent entry-level Maserati for the enthusiast who enjoys working on the car himself and has a family. All Quattroporte Is were equipped with factory air conditioning. Most Quattroporte parts are readily available; lots of used parts, including body parts, are also readily available, as nearly 1,500 cars were made.

Quattroporte II

The Quattroporte II, with coachwork by Bertone, was the brainchild of the then-new Citroen-Maserati management. Developed in the early '70s, and shown at the 1974 November Turin Auto Show, the Quattroporte II never made it into volume production. With approximately 10 cars built, the project was put on the back burner during the financial crisis of 1975 and ultimately killed by the new DeTomaso management.

Equipped with the Merak/Citroen SM 3-liter V-6 engine, it was the first and, one hopes, the last, front-wheel-drive Maserati GT car. It was essentially a Citroen-SM with Italian coachwork. It's not known for sure, but it probably was the work of Marcello Gandini, who is the father of all those great Bertone-bodied Lamborghinis. It is possible that the sheer uniqueness of these virtually prototype vehicles could one day in the future make them quite desirable. Price in today's market shouldn't exceed $25,000, although importing the car into the US would be extremely difficult as none of them were US legal.

Mexico

The replacement for the 5000 GT 2+2 (after 32 cars) came in the form of the Mexico, named after the racing success of John Surtees at the 1966 Mexican Grand Prix, at the wheel of the V-12-powered Cooper-Maserati.

The Mexico was a luxurious 2+2, designed by Vignale and introduced at the 1966 Turin Auto Show. Approximately 250 cars were produced. The Mexico was initially equipped with a 4.2-liter V-8, driving through a ZF transmission, and live rear axle. The interior was fitted with a beautiful wood dash and window trim. The lovely Connolly leather interior featured thick Wilton wool carpets, and all cars were air conditioned. Later Mexicos were fitted with 4.7-liter engines, and a few even made it off the assembly line with the 4.9-liter engine. Power steering was an option (an important one); if you can find one with power steering you are better off. Although standard steering cars can be a little bit heavy in parking situations, on balance they have good road feel and offer simplicity.

Maserati Mexico   *Francis Mandarano Photo*

Conservative in styling, even by today's standards, the Mexico has a large greenhouse and is well proportioned. The rear seats are large and can actually accommodate two adults in relative comfort over long distances - unlike most 2 + 2 cars. In fact, the factory described the Mexico as a "4-posti" car.

On the collectibility scale, the Mexico falls somewhere between the four-door Quattroporte and the Indy. Really superb examples can be had in the $40,000 range with lesser-condition cars going down from there. Four-place cars just don't have the collectibililty of the two seaters or the spyders. However, the Mexico can be a lot of fun to own and drive with a front-end cost of half what you would expect to pay for the same condition two seater.

Ghibli

The Ghibli, named after a hot desert wind that blows across the Sahara desert, was first introduced at the 1966 Turin Auto Show where it created a sensation. Penned by the young maestro Giorgetto Giugiaro while still at Ghia, the Ghibli is perhaps the most famous of all Maserati GT cars. And, it is certainly the most successful and collectible.

Maserati Ghibli   *Francis Mandarano Photo*

A genuine two seat sports car with a long hood and low roof-line profile, the Ghibli strikes an aggressive, yet elegant pose. Because of the low profile of the hood, that beautiful 4.7-liter engine that had been fitted to the Quattroportes and Mexicos was now re-engineered to accept a dry sump oiling system to reduce the overall height of the engine. To accommodate the 13 + quarts of oil, an external oil tank was mounted in the front of the engine and was fed by two hoses.

First series Ghiblis were equipped with 4.7-liter engines fed by four 40DCNL5 carburetors. The power was transmitted through the

German built ZF S5 325 transmission and on to a Salisbury live rear axle, with multiple ratios being offered. Early cars were also equipped with Smith instruments, manual steering, radiator cooling fans mounted in front of the radiator, toggle-type accessory switches, and a dual Girling booster braking system.

The second series cars got improvements such as tilt and telescopic steering wheel, a new induction system featuring 42DCNF Weber carburetors, a more advanced cooling system with a single thermostat, a Bonaldi power brake booster, as opposed to the two Girling brake boosters, and, on some cars, we find the 4.9-liter SS engine option.

The 4.7-liter blocks were stamped with one S and the 4.9-liter engines were stamped with two Ss. It's simply a quick and easy visual mark to ascertain the size of the engine, as that information is not always available in the chassis number except where the numeral 4.9 is inserted. The only difference between an "SS" car and a non-"SS" car is that 2/10ths of a liter. An inspection of the engine serial number will clearly reveal whether it is a 4.9 liter SS or not. Expect to pay 10-20% more for a 4.9 SS Ghibli over a comparable 4.7-liter Ghibli.

Mechanically the Ghibli is bullet proof with the exception of the dry-sump oiling system. Its reservoir contains screens that filter the oil. These can clog over time, resulting in oil starvation to the engine. Relatively simple diagnosis can be performed by just accelerating in the car. If upon acceleration you see a fluctuation of oil pressure, or the oil pressure needle drops back, that is a sure indication that the engine is being oil-starved. The solution is not an expensive one; simply remove the oil reservoir canister and phone the Maserati Club International (206-455-4449) for instructions.

Over the period from 1967 through 1974, approximately 1100 Ghibli coupes were built. Of those 1100, some 200-270 of them were SS cars, equipped with 4.9-liter engines. Prices of good condition, #2 quality, Ghibli coupes run approximately $44-55,000 in today's market. Add another 10-20% for SS versions.

The Ghibli Spyder

It was only natural with the huge success of the coupe that Maserati would request Ghia to submit a design proposal for a spyder. First shown at the 1968 Turin Auto Show, the spyder version was a huge success. Commonly referred to as, "The most beautiful sports car ever built", its proportions and styling are absolutely stunning, even by today's standards. Approximately 124 Ghibli spyders were built, and of that number, approximately 40 were SS cars. A gorgeous fitted hard top was available, and approximately 25 cars left the factory with this hard top in place. A 4.7-liter Ghibli spyder in superb condition will fetch approximately $160,000 in today's market with the equivalent SS version bringing 10-20% more. Prepare to spend up to $10,000 for a factory-fitted hard top - if you can find one!

Indy

At the 1969 Geneva Auto Show, Maserati introduced the all-new Indy, designed by Vignale. The name Indy came from Wilbur Shaw's 1939 and 1940 back-to-back wins at the Indianapolis 500 in the Maserati 8CTF. Approximately 1044 cars were produced over a six-year period beginning in 1969. They're a genuine 2+2 with room enough for four adults to travel over long distances in comfort. Initial Indys were equipped with the 260 hp, four-cam V-8 engine carried over from the Mexico and Quattroporte I cars, with upgraded 42DCNF Weber carburetors and an all-new intake manifold. New heads were developed that featured one water passage per head. One large thermostat equals 42DCNF carburetors and late style heads; two small thermostats indicate 38DCNL5 or 40DCNL5 Webers and early heads.

Let's examine the first series. They were generally of 4.2-liters, without power steering and equipped with an S520, all-aluminum, ZF transmission. The second series Indy came equipped with an all-new dash layout with instruments laid out above the shifter in a row. Power steering was now standard as were other cosmetic improvements. Indy's strong points include a rating of excellent in body construction. In the MIE workshop, we have worked on no less than 25 Indys, and in each case we have noticed a very high degree of assembly quality. The fit and finish is decisively better than other Maseratis. In fact, if I had to say which car was built the best, I would have to give the Indy the nudge. The detail level is phenomenal.

The Indy is a very nice car to drive in that its seating position is unlike any other. The hood line is very low, and you have an excellent command of the road. When equipped with the 4.7 and 4.9-liter variants, the Indy can produce some blood rushing excitement. Compared with the Ghibli, the Indy is a bargain. Any Indy in good condition would be a fun car to own. There are no real vices, except for rust and previous poor maintenance. Good Indys, at this moment, can be had in the $35-45,000 range.

Maserati Bora   *MIE Archive Photo*

Bora

As 1970 approached, the leading designers were turning towards mid-engine placement and Maserati wasn't about to be left in the dust. Giorgetto Giugiaro at his newly formed Ital Design was commissioned to do a study for a mid-engined car. What he came up with turned out to be the sensation of the 1971 Geneva Auto Show where the Bora was first displayed.

In collaboration with his French colleagues at Citroen, Sig. Guilio Alfieri, the masterful engineer who had been with Maserati since the days of the 250F back in 1954, put together a two-place rocketship with brakes that could stop on a dime and give you change! It's as if a giant hand comes out of the sky and grabs the car. Not only does the steering wheel telescope and tilt, but the seat can be raised quietly by hydraulic servos. And, for the first time in any production car, the pedal cluster can be moved fore and aft hydraulically with a touch of a switch. You didn't just get into a Bora and drive away, you were fitted to the Bora and blasted away. The power is sensational, the feeling of safety is remarkable.

There were three series of Boras; the first were Europe-only cars that did not make it to these shores. The second series cars came to us equipped with one stainless steel bumper in front and the same rear treatment as the European cars. The third series of cars came to us equipped with a large rubber bumper in both front and rear, and dual exhausts exiting out of the lower valance. All interiors were the same, except for the European steering wheel verses the USA steering wheel, and all cars were equipped with the same wheels and hub caps except for the final cars which were sans hub caps.

Approximately 340 Boras were built between 1972 and 1978. That's not very many, therefore, the Bora is very collectible. It's the only Maserati sports car with a mid-engine V-8 (remember its little brother Merak had the V-6 built for Citroen). Nice Boras can currently be had in the $60-70,000 range.

Merak

Part of the reason Citroen bought Maserati was so they could use their engine designing and building technology to produce an exotic engine for their upscale Citroen SM, of which over 10,000 cars were eventually built. In the early '70s Maserati was mass-producing these V-6 engines, so the management felt it was only reasonable to produce a scaled-down Bora variant called Merak to make use of this new V-6 engine. The design-wise Citroen management again assigned the task to Giorgetto Giugiaro of Ital Design, who produced a strikingly similar car. In fact, from the doors forward, they were the same. The 2.7-liter SM engine was bored out to 3 liters and installed in the Merak, in a north and south position, coupled to a Citroen five-speed transmission.

These cars are light and well balanced. I would go so far as to say the Merak is the best handling modern Maserati GT car; in fact, I consider the 1977 and later Merak SS cars to be one of the great, all time, every day Maserati drivers. The Italianized "SS" is sans-Citroen hydraulics and equipped with the Bora-style dash. It has all the latest horsepower and cosmetic modifications and is really a first-rate driver. Again, three different variants were produced: First series, Citroen hydraulics, Citroen style dash; second series European version with the squared off dash; third series, Bora style dash and no Citroen hydraulics.

When inspecting a Merak for possible purchase, be sure to check the camshaft chains. The factory recommends these be changed every 35-40,000 miles. In a lot of cases where the upper chains have been changed, the more difficult lower one has not, and therefore has become very sloppy. A loose lower chain is a bargaining point. The bad rap on the Merak engine is largely undeserved. The key to engine life is setting them up properly the first time, and then maintaining them on a regular basis. Beginning in 1972 and ending in 1983, over 2500 Meraks were produced, by far the largest number of any Maserati GT car to date. You can find excellent examples for $35,000 to $45,000.

Khamsin

First shown at the 1972 Turin Auto Show, the Khamsin was a marvelous creation from the house of Bertone, and was the first front engine GT car to be developed entirely by the Citroen management. Penned by Marcello Gandini in the prime of his career, the Khamsin remains as beautiful today as it was 20 years ago when it was first conceived.

Commonly referred to as "the last great Maserati GT car", the Khamsin represents the total accumulation of Maserati knowledge up to the point of its creation. By supercar standards, it is absolutely brilliant. It's equipped with the Citroen-patented hydraulic circuitry which controls not only the brakes, but the headlight buckets, the seat position, the power steering and the clutch. For example, the clutch is not only hydraulically actuated, but it is hydraulically assisted, just enough to give you good pedal feel. The incredible power steering will turn the car in a circle tighter than a car half its size and, upon reaching speeds of 50-60 mph, a governor-hardener, driven off the rear half shafts, firms the steering up so it has a non-power steering feel. It's just exactly what you would want at any speed between 60-150 mph.

The Khamsin was obviously developed to replace the Ghibli. It is as if you took thirty guys and gave them a Ghibli and said, "let's hot-rod this Ghibli anyway we can". What they produced used the 4.9-liter SS engine, the big ZF S5-24-3 transmission driving through an independent rear suspension - which in itself is a marvelous work of art. Consider this: the rear suspension is incorporated into its own rear sub-frame; this sub-frame is mounted on rubber bushings that attach to the body, creating somewhat of a buffer for road noise. Not only does it have large inboard rear disc brakes, but four-coil-over shock absorbers, unequal length A-arms and an anti-roll bar.

Over the period 1972 - 1982, approximately 450 Khamsins were built. Collectible? Very much so. A Khamsin will really turn people's heads wherever it appears. Current prices range from $35,000 to 40,000.

Kyalami

Shortly after Sig. DeTomaso's take over of Maserati in 1975, he sent one of his Tom Tjaarda-designed Longchamps to Sig. Frua in Torino for a freshening up. Frua did a marvelous job on this coupe, providing a grille and frontal area that had a strong family resemblance to his earlier Quattroporte and, of course, the Vignale Mexico. The Kyalami truly became the evolution of the Mexico, and is named for the racing success Maserati enjoyed at the South African Grand Prix. This would be the last Maserati Pietro Frua would do, as he died shortly thereafter. He produced a luxurious, but simple 2+2 - a car I've dubbed the two door Quattroporte. The running gear would all be used later in the new Quattroporte III. The tried and true 4.2-liter, four-cam, Maserati V8 is coupled to the big ZF S5 24-3 transmission, and power is transferred to the independently-sprung rear end, featuring in-board brakes and giant aluminum outer hubs.

It's conservative in styling, yet classical in execution, very Italian, very impressive. Consider the 225 70 VR 15 Michelin XWX mounted on the Campagnolo 7 1/2-inch-wide wheel. No complicated fuel injection system, just simple Weber carburetors. There are really no weak points in the Kyalami; it's a hard-charging, trouble-free thoroughbred. Collectible? Very much so, because of the very limited number produced and the fact that so few exist in the US. None were certified or officially sold into the states, but approximately ten to fifteen Kyalamis have found their way into the US, making them a very rare car in this country. These facts alone would indicate that this is a car worth considering. Over an eight-year period, the factory produced no more than 250 Kyalamis, Prices today (August of 1991) run in the $25-35,000 range for a nice original Kyalami, with top prices being fetched for the 4.9-liter cars.

Quattroporte III

After the success of the Kyalami transformation, DeTomaso again asked Giorgetto Giugiaro of Ital Design to design a new Maserati saloon. A working prototype first shown at the 1976 Torino show was quickly recognized for its classical, elegant, Italian styling. It also became known as the car with "the interior" that was far better than anything else on the market. Some even called it the "greatest interior in the world," a title which it holds to this day. With an abundance of real briarwood and no less than eight cowhides transformed into the finest Florentine leather you will find, the Quattroporte interior is a palatial palace ready to engulf you in luxury and serenity. It is the first Maserati to be fully tooled, that is to say, it is not a hand built car. In fact, it was produced at the Innocenti plant in Milan, a 40-acre manufacturing facility that DeTomaso had acquired earlier to produce mini cars.

At 4750 pounds, it's not a light-weight, but don't be fooled. It has plenty of get up and go. The 4.9-liter, four-cam aluminum V8, now producing about 290 horsepower, has plenty of what it takes to move the Quattroporte along at autostrada speeds in comfort and style. Under the hood, the 4.9 liter V8 that we first saw in the Quattraporte I introduced in 1963, has evolved into its final form. Upgrades include a new water pump, a vacuum pump driven off the intake cam, electronic ignition and all the emission equipment necessary for certification into the US market. The Quattroporte is a car that you can drive and use on an everyday basis. Collectible? In the long term yes, short term no. But, it probably won't depreciate much if properly maintained. At some point in the future, it could become a sought after classic. Does it matter if the car is early or late? Not really. Get the Quattroporte that is in the best condition. Remember, less than 3,000 of these were produced for world-wide consumption. Prices are excellent, as low-mileage Quattroportes can be had in the $18-24,000 range.

Biturbo

On December 14, 1981, precisely 67 years after Alfieri Maserati founded the Maserati Company in Bologna, Signor DeTomaso introduced the long awaited Maserati for the masses. The Biturbo (pronounced Bee-turbo) had a V6 twin-turbo-charged 2.5-liter engine with a single Weber carburetor driving through a ZF transmission. The Biturbo is about the size of a BMW 320i, and has many features borrowed from the BMW including the front and rear suspension and steering. There the resemblance ends, for the interior is very luxurious. Cars destined for the US had leather seat faces and matching Naugahyde to cover the rest of the interior. Very nice, very Italian. The first Biturbos were introduced to the USA in 1984. Incidentally, issue number 51 of Viale Ciro Menotti contains an excellent Biturbo owners' survey including good points, bad points, and how the owners feel about their Biturbos. For 1986 a four-door Biturbo was added to the line numbered the 425: four for four doors, and two five for 2.5-liter. Also in 1986, a stylish spyder by Zagato was added to the line, available with automatic transmission only and a blue convertible top. For 1987, fuel injection was added, which turned the car into a completely different animal.

Maserati Biturbo   *Pete Coltrin Photo*

After the spyder came the Biturbo E model, the first of several variants, to which West Coast distributor Kjell Quale added Spearco intercoolers and other accessories. Approximately 250 E models were sold. The next cars we saw in the US were the 425 I, the Biturbo Si, and the spyder. All three were fuel-injected, but basically the same car as before. In 1987, we got the 430, the new spyder and the 228. The 430 was a 425 with new sheet metal, the engine enlarged to 2.8 liters, quad exhaust, 15-inch wheels, twin air-to-air intercoolers and a lovely new interior. The new 1988 spyder also got the 2.8-liter engine as well as all of the above features. The 228, built on the 430 chassis, was wider and stouter with softer lines. It also came equipped with the quad-exhaust, 2.8-liter engine, air-to-air intercoolers, 15-inch wheels, etc. Only 97 228s were imported into the US, and at $57,000 they were not big sellers.

Of all the Biturbo variants, the 228 has the best prospect of becoming a collector car. In fact, all the Biturbos built after 1988 have extremely high quality built in. When shopping for a Biturbo, be sure to consider the later cars first. For a few extra thousand dollars in up-front cost, they are vastly superior in build-quality, appointments and freedom from design faults.

What to look for in purchasing a Biturbo? Be sure to drive it to test the clutch. If it's slipping, it will cost about $750 to fix. If you have time, disconnect the high-pressure hose from the turbos to the carburetor plenum. If you find oil deposits inside, chances are the turbo's ready to fail. Prices range from $640-700 for a rebuilt turbo. With the engine idling, remove the oil cap from the left and then the right hand cam covers, and look in with a flashlight. If you see plenty of oil splashing around, everything is OK. However, if you find there isn't much oil splashing around, it's a sign the bronze oil filters are clogged with coke deposits. This restricts the oil flow to the cams, causing them to seize, bending valves, breaking the timing belt, and causing about $3,000 worth of damage. These faults are repairable, but recognizing them ahead of time will prevent disaster and will give you bargaining leverage.

During your test drive, shift to second gear and floor the throttle. If while the tachometer passes the 5000 mark the boost needle is up well into the yellow, the car is performing as it should. If the boost needle doesn't get to the yellow, the car is not boosting correctly and needs service. Is the Biturbo collectible? Probably not. Is it a lot of fun? Absolutely! You get a big bang for the buck. Prices of 1984 and 1985 Biturbo coupes currently run in the $6-8,000 range. 1987 Si's sell for $9-12,000. 425s go for $10,000. 1986 spyders will cost $11-14,000. 1989 and 1990 spyders are $22-26,000.

1989 and 1990 430s will cost $22-26,000, and 228s bring $25-29,000. All of these offer excellent value for money in a semi-thoroughbred rocketship with classic Italian styling.

PERILS TO WATCH OUT FOR

As quality restoration is extremely difficult to find and very expensive (remember it took 9,600 hours to restore last year's Pebble Beach winning Bugatti owned by Ralph Lauren), be sure to check any car over carefully. If it hasn't been well cared for there can be a multitude of things wrong that need to be completely replaced (not overhauled but replaced).

The weak point with all Maseratis is rust. Prepare for rust, lots of rust; these cars were usually driven and, if they sat outside and were washed, they would rust. Check everything - floor pans, inner fender panels - you name it. Door panels should be removed and the inside of the doors inspected. Rocker panels and the trunk bottom are other areas to inspect. Look for rust in the rocker panels, doors, hood and trunk area, and braking system. Put a prospective purchase up on a hoist and poke around with a screwdriver. If you don't find any rust, buy the car instantly because it will indeed be a rare example.

The electrics, despite what people say, are usually pretty simple and are just a matter of disassembly, cleaning and reassembly (cleaning contacts, etc). Carbureted cars are more desirable than the Lucas-fuel-injected models.

Also watch out for frozen brake boosters, rusty brake lines and pitted or rusted brake caliper pistons. Because the cars tend to sit around a lot, moisture condenses into water in the brake lines and produces pitting and rusting. The Girling/Lucas braking system, if not rebuilt and used, can store lots of hidden problems, seized brake boosters that lock up the brakes, and, of course, a pitted and rusting master cylinder. When purchasing a Maserati that hasn't been driven regularly, be prepared to completely rebuild the brake system (which can cost from $2,000 upward).

WHERE TO GET EXPERT HELP

A serious interest in Maseratis will require the eventual help of both fellow enthusiasts and professionals. A good start is to join the club that caters to the marque.

Maserati Club International
Box 772
Mercer Island, Washington   98040

This 3,500-member club organized in 1976 publishes a slick quarterly magazine <u>Viale Ciro Menotti</u> that carries information, free ads for members, technical help and problem solving, and <u>Maserati Market Letter</u>, which carries ads and current market values for all Maserati models.

WHERE TO GET PARTS

MIE
2120 116th Avenue NE
Bellevue, Washington 98004
206-455-4449, fax 206-646-5458

ABOUT THE AUTHOR

In 1974, Francis Mandarano acquired his first Maserati, a 3500 GTI which he still owns to this day. Early in his ownership, his frustration in locating parts and information to rebuild the car led him and his future wife Janet to found the Maserati Club International, which today has over 3500 members in 39 countries. The Mandaranos have owned examples of virtually every Maserati GT car produced. Their current collection consists of their first 3500 GT Coupe, a Ghibli spyder, the 1959 3500 GT Bertone prototype, a Kyalami, an A6GCS and five vintage Maserati motorcycles, including a very rare 50cc "racing frog". As publisher of Viale Ciro Menotti, a magazine for Maserati owners and enthusiasts, Francis has authored over 75 technical and historical articles about the marque.

YEAR	LINE	Relative Condition: Worse ↔ Better		
		❸	❷	❶
1957–1964	3500GT/GTI Coupe	30000	40000	48000
1957–1964	3500GT/GTI Vignale Spyder	150000	175000	195000
1962–1966	Sebring Series I Coupe	33000	41000	48000
1965–1966	Sebring Series II Coupe	33000	44000	54000
1963–1970	Mistral Coupe	32000	38000	45000
1964–1970	Mistral Spyder	105000	135000	160000
1963–1969	Quattro Porte 4Dr Sedan	12500	17500	24500
1965–1968	Mexico Coupe	21000	30000	36000
1967–1973	Ghibli Coupe	48000	62000	74000
1969–1972	Ghibli Spyder	155000	175000	20000
1963–1974	Indy Coupe	28000	34000	40000
1974–1980	Khamsin Coupe	33000	40000	48000
1971–1980	Bora Coupe	55000	68000	85000
1972–1977	Merak Coupe	22000	29000	34000
1977–1980	Merak SS Coupe	25000	33000	37000

MERCEDES-BENZ

BY BILL SIURU

THE CAR OF THE STAR

To many of the uninitiated, every car that wears a silver tri-pointed star is a mega-buck collectible, or at least a potential one. However, a trip to Germany, or many other foreign countries, for that matter, will soon bring home the fact that outside of the US, while the name Mercedes-Benz might be respected, it is not necessarily revered. For every collectible Mercedes-Benz, the company has produced thousands of rather mundane, though well-built and rugged, sedans and station wagons that serve as family cars, police cars, taxis and even cars of choice for terrorists.

While recent vintage Mercedes-Benz gasoline and diesel sedans and many older ones make good, not great, daily drivers and used cars, they will never become prime collectibles. But, well maintained transportation cars will retain their values like models from no other marque. Of course, there also many Mercedes-Benz models that are "blue chip" collectibles.

HISTORY OF THE MARQUE

In 1886, Karl Benz and Gottlieb Daimler, quite independently, developed automobiles. Benz's was a three-wheeler, Daimler's a converted four-wheel horse-drawn carriage. While neither pioneer can be credited with "inventing" the car, both were the first to build gasoline power vehicles that worked. The two automakers continued on their separate paths. They barely knew each other, for over a quarter century building cars under the Firma Benz & Cie, Rheinische Automobil und Motorenfabrik AG and Daimler Motoren Gesellschaft labels before they merged in 1926 to form Daimler-Benz AG. While Karl Benz was around to see the merger, Gottlieb Daimler had died in 1900.

In 1901, the name Mercedes was first used on cars produced by Daimler. The name honored Mercedes Jellinek, the daughter of

Emil Jellinek, a wealthy Austrian banker, businessman and diplomat who played a major role in Daimler's early years as a financial backer, director, distributor and motorsports enthusiast. The familiar three-point star first appeared on a Mercedes car in the early 1900s and in 1923 the star was encircled by a ring and became a patented radiator mascot. The trademark was further enhanced with laurel wreath and the words "Mercedes-Benz" to signify the 1926 merger.

Almost from the start, both Benz and Daimler were heavily involved in racing. The long Mercedes-Benz motorsports story could fill books, and indeed has. For instance, the early Blitzen Benz held the world's speed record for an amazing 15 years from 1909 with an incredible 127.4 mph increasing appropriately to hold on to the record until 1924. Both Benz and Mercedes cars were frequent winners at race tracks throughout Europe and a Mercedes driven by Ralph DePalma won the Indianapolis 500 in 1915.

In 1923, Daimler hired a brilliant engineer by the name of Ferdinand Porsche to head the company's design team. Porsche stayed on through the merger and would have a major influence on the marque's products in the prewar years.

The late 1920s and 1930s were the golden years for Mercedes-Benz. Grand Prix racing, especially in the late 1930s, was dominated by the Mercedes-Benz "Silver Arrows" race cars, such as the W25, W125, W154 and W163 driven by likes of Rudolf Caracciola, Hermann Lang and Manfred von Brauchitsch. On the consumer side, Mercedes-Benz was continuously developing and marketing its long line of high-performance, advanced-technology luxury sports cars like the S/SS/SSK/SSLK series, 500K and 540K of prewar fame. The "K" stood for "mit Kompressor" since Mercedes-Benz was a leader in using superchargers in automobiles.

While the race cars and luxury cars got most of the limelight, Mercedes-Benz also produced a variety of lower-priced vehicles including the rear-engined 130 Daimler-Benz "people's car" that preceded the Volkswagen. Mercedes-Benz has also been the continuous world leader in diesel-powered cars since offering the world's first one, the 260D, in 1936. Throughout its history, cars have represented only a part of Daimler-Benz product lines, since it is a major worldwide supplier of trucks and buses, industrial and marine engines, and, periodically, aircraft engines.

Even though some 80 percent of Daimler-Benz was destroyed during World War II, recovery was remarkably rapid. By 1946, Mercedes-Benz had reintroduced its prewar 170V model. In 1951, Mercedes-Benz re-entered the luxury car market with its 300-series of sedans, coupes, cabriolets and four-door convertibles. In 1953, Mercedes-Benz brought out its first completely new postwar models, the four-cylinder 180 followed shortly by the six-cylinder 220s that both featured unitized bodies. These were the first Mercedes-Benz to be imported into the US in serious quantities.

MERCEDES-BENZ SL MODELS

300SL Gullwing Coupe and Roadster

The Mercedes-Benz SL series started with the legendary 300SL gullwing coupe. The 300SL started life as a thoroughbred race car, as Silver Arrows were again making their presence known in racing circles starting in 1952. Indeed, the 300SL is the only SL with a serious racing history. In 1952, Mercedes-Benz dazzled the motorsports world with a string of victories with 300SLs, including a first and second in the 1952 LeMans 24 hour race, plus wins in the Carrera Panamericana (the Mexican Road Race), the Grand Prix of Bern and the "Grand Jubilee" at Nurburgring. Unfortunately, Mercedes-Benz's revived involvement in world-class racing was brief. It disbanded its racing team after Pierre Levegh's 300SLR crashed into the grandstand at LeMans in 1955, resulting in the worst accident in motorsports history.

SL stands for Sport Leicht, or Sport Light in English. The 300SL's lightness was obtained from a stiff, but very light, multitube chassis made of thin welded steel tubing formed into a lattice-type stress-bearing structure. The frame weighed a mere 180 pounds. A thin outer skin covered this framework, forming the aerodynamically efficient body. To further keep weight down, the 300SLs used an aluminum hood, rocker panels, hood, trunklid and all-aluminum body. 300SLs could be ordered for competition duty.

Clockwise from lower right: 300SL gulling,   MBNA Photo
300SL roadster, 190SL, 280SL, 450SL

The 300SL was the first Mercedes-Benz production car that did not use the characteristic upright grille, but pioneered the alternate oval, tri-star grille that has been used on the more sporting Mercedes-Benz models ever since. Other unique styling features included "eyebrows" over the wheel wells, "power bulges" in the hood, and the functional louvers in the front fenders and in the rear of the roof. Finally, there were the unique gullwing opening doors that were dictated by the need to maintain the space frame's structural integrity, ruling out cutouts for full length doors. Doors were required by the FIA race sanctioning body.

Max Hoffman, the premier early car importer, convinced Mercedes-Benz that they should produce a road going version of the 300SL, backing up his demand with an order for 1000 cars. The road-going 300SL made its debut at the 1954 New York Auto Show. The production SLs retained most of the features found on the racing version, including the gullwing doors. However, unlike the racers that used triple Solex carburetors on the six-cylinder, 3-liter engine, the production 300 SL used a Bosch mechanical fuel injection system, earning it a place in automotive history as the first production car to offer fuel injection. The engine was inclined in the engine compartment to reduce hood height. Some 1,445 gullwings were eventually produced between 1954 and 1957.

The more refined 300SL roadster, which could be ordered with a removable steel top as well as a soft top, was offered first in 1957, and a total of 1,858 300SL roadsters were produced before production ended in 1963. This 300SL used a greatly revised independent swing rear axle that resulted in safer, better handling than the earlier gullwing's race-bred swing rear axle setup. And, while the 300SL used the ultimate in 1950s brake technology with its servo-boosted, aluminum, radially-finned brakes, they are no match for four-wheel disc brakes, which were finally made available on the 300SL roadster in 1963. The 240-horsepower engine could push the 2850 pound (2950 pounds for the roadster) to a respectable 145 mph.

190SL

The next SL was aimed at a greater segment of the buying public. The smaller 190SL was equipped with a hopped-up version of the the 1.9 liter four-cylinder, single-over-head camshaft used in the 190 series of sedans. The engine with twin Solex carburetors and 105 horsepower engine would propel the 2550 pound 190SL to nearly 110 mph. The 190SL used unibody construction. Much of the 190SL styling, including the fender eyebrows, was definitely inspired by the 190SL's bigger brother, the 300SL. While performance was decent, the 190SL was more luxury-sports car than racing-sports car. Even so, the 190SL had four-wheel independent suspension and aluminum doors, trunk and hood to keep the weight down. Brakes were still drums all around. A total of 25,881 190SLs were produced from 1955 through 1963.

230SL/250SL/280SL

The 230SL was introduced in 1963 as a replacement for both the 190SL and 300SL. Its most distinguishing feature was the pagoda-shaped removable hardtop. Initially, the 230SL used a fuel-injected 2.3-liter SOHC six that produced 150 horsepower, giving a top speed of 125 mph. In 1966, the displacement was increased to 2.5 liters, and the designation was changed to 250SL accordingly, but horsepower remained the same. The 280SL appeared in 1968, when the engine displacement was increased to 2.8 liters and the horsepower was now 170. Between 1963 and 1971, 49,912 230/250/280SLs were produced, 19,831 ('63-'67 230SL), 5196 ('67-'68 250SL), and 23,885 ('68-'71 280SL).

While the 230SL used disc/drum brakes, the 250SL and 280SL featured four-wheel disc brakes. All three versions were available with either a four or five-speed manual transmission; most all were fitted with a four-speed automatic transmission. This, plus amenities like air-conditioning, more luxurious interiors, power steering and other power options, portend the SL's evolution from sports car to luxury grand touring car with the next evolution of the SL series. The 280SL would be the last Mercedes-Benz sports car to use the venerable swing rear axle.

350SL/450SL/380SL/500SL/560SL

On August 4, 1989, a signal-red Mercedes-Benz 500SL rolled off the Mercedes-Benz's Sindelfingen assembly line, the last of a breed. After 18 years of production of the 350SL/450SL/380SL/ 500SL/560SL series with a total of 237,287 produced, it was time for a changing of the guard. The replacement was, of course, the new 300/500SL with all its "leading edge" technology. Oh yes, this last Mercedes-Benz R107 (Mercedes-Benz's internal designation for the series) was not destined for a dealership, but for a place of honor in the Mercedes-Benz Museum in Stuttgart.

Mercedes-Benz 450 SL   *MBNA Photo*

The-all new 350SL first appeared in the fall of 1971 as a 1972 model. The 350SL was the first SL to use the Mercedes-Benz overhead cam V-8. And, while the Europeans got a 3.5-liter V-8, a 4.5-liter V-8 was sold in the US, even though it was designated the 350SL until 1973, when it was correctly redesignated the 450SL. The 4.5-liter engine produced 190 horsepower.

While the R107 series was produced for an incredible 18 years, there were continual modifications. In 1974, US models got larger, DOT-mandated bumpers (hardly an improvement). Major updates for 1976 included CSI mechanical fuel injection, hydraulic valve adjustment, and a two-way catalytic converter. Automatic climate control came in 1977. The last year for the 450SL was 1980. For 1981, there was an all-aluminum 3.8-liter 155-horsepower V-8 to replace the cast-iron 4.5-liter powerplant, and the designation became the 380SL. In 1986, to compete with "grey market" 500SL that were being imported, Mercedes-Benz of North America offered the 560 SL fitted with a 227-horsepower, 5.6-liter, all-aluminum V-8. The 560SL also received larger brakes, wheels and tires, plus "retuning" of the suspension. As the model approached the end of its life, features such as limited-slip differential, rear-axle torque compensation, anti-lock brakes, functional air dam, driver's side airbag, and anti-theft alarm were added as standard equipment. The car grew in weight to nearly 2 tons, and the title SL for "sport leicht" no longer seemed appropriate. While far from a "wind-in-your-face" sports car, the SL cannot be beat as a high-speed, grand touring car for two. Incidently, the Europeans got versions not only with a 4.2 and 5.0-liter V-8, but also a 2.8 and 3.0- liter six-cylinder. Of the 237,287 of the R107 SLs produced, 153,244, or nearly 65 percent, were officially sold in North America.

350SLC/380SLC/450SLC

For the first decade of the R107 roadster's life, there was a companion SLC model that had much of the SL's looks and most of its mechanical features. The SLC could be considered a "stretched" version of the SL roadster, since it was created from the SL by adding some 14 inches to the SL's wheelbase and overall length. Since all the additional stretch came between the wheels, the interior was increased so the SLC had a real rear seat that could carry four people in comfort. The most distinctive part of the modified design was the louvers added in the rear window area. The extra letter stood for "Sports Leicht Coupe". The initial 280SLC appeared late in the 1971 model year.

The term leicht, or "light," was a bit of a misnomer since the cars approached the two-ton level. While all SLCs were built as hardtop coupes, a few were converted to convertibles by outside coachbuilders. The SLC's design changed little during the car's production life, which ran from 1971 through 1981. The most significant change, at least on American-destined cars, were the 5-mph fed-bumpers that appeared in 1974, adding almost ten inches in length over their foreign brothers. After producing 62,888 SLCs, the model was superseded by 380SEC/500SEC coupes.

Roughly three SL roadsters were produced for every SLC coupe.

Like the SL roadsters, a variety of engines were fitted in the SLC coupes, in most cases, the same ones. The initial model was the 350SLC that featured a 3.5-liter V-8. The American version used a larger 4.5-liter V-8, but, unlike the 350SL 4.5 for Americans, the coupe was always designated the 450SLC. While the 350SL came with either a four-speed or automatic transmission, the American 450SLCs were fitted with automatic transmissions, plus a full line of luxury items like air conditioning, power brakes and power steering, central locking, stereo radio, leather upholstery and more. There was also a European version of the 450SLC with considerably better performance and less weight.

Mercedes-Benz 450SLC   *MBNA Photo*

For 1978, Mercedes-Benz's new 5.0 aluminum V-8 was installed in the SLC to create the 450SLC 5.0. To further reduce weight, light alloy wheels, hood and trunk were used, which shaved off about 220 pounds. On most cars, plastic spoilers were added to both the front and rear to improve aerodynamic efficiency a bit. Anti-lock braking (ABS) was available on the 450SLC 5.0. After 1980, the model was designated the 500SLC and a four-speed automatic replaced the previously used three-speed automatic. Mercedes-Benz of North America did not import the 5-liter SLCs.

Instead, we got the 380SL that used another new lightweight V-8 which produced 155 horsepower and used a four-speed automatic. For the European market after 1974, there was the 280SLC with a 2746 cc, six-cylinder, DOHC engine. The 280SLC was the only SLC that could be ordered with a five-speed manual transmission.

COLLECTIBLE SEDANS

300/300b/300c/300d

The 300 series that appeared first in 1951 demonstrated that Mercedes-Benz was well on its way to re-establishing its pre-war level of excellence in both engineering and workmanship. While styling of these luxury four-door sedans and convertibles may not be exactly beautiful, they are definitely impressive. The 2996 cc six-cylinder overhead-cam engine that produced between 115 and 160 horsepower in the 300 sedans would soon evolve into the 240 horsepower powerplant for 300SL gullwing racers and road cars. The 300c, produced between 1955 and 1957, used a slightly more powerful engine (125 horsepower) and an automatic transmission was now optional.

The 300d that was introduced in 1957 received a major facelift that included more modern rear fenders and, in keeping up with the rest of the automobile industry, it became a four-door hardtop. Under the 300d's hood, the 3-liter engine now used Bosch mechanical fuel injection like the 300SL, and power was up to 160 horsepower. Part of the 300's advanced technology included four-wheel independent suspension with the height of the rear controlled electrically from the driver's seat via auxiliary torsion bars. Besides the four-door "limousine", the 300s came as an even more impressive four-door convertible. The 300 series was produced in rather small quantities with some 10,723 made between 1951 and 1962, with the convertible representing only a small portion of the total produced.

Type 600

The 2677 "Grosser" 600 Mercedes-Benz produced between 1963 and 1981 were hand-built to order and arguably the "world's most luxurious limousines." They definitely could compete with anything from Rolls-Royce in luxury and looks, and could out-perform and out-handle anything the competition had to offer. These huge cars came in several versions including a standard-wheelbase (126 inch) limousine, four-door longer wheelbase (153.5 inch) six door "Pullman" limousine, and the rare "landaulette" versions with a fold-down rear fabric rear section for duty in parades and state functions. Being handcrafted, there are many "one-offs" including a couple of 600 two-door coupes.

Mercedes-Benz 600   *MBNA Photo*

The 600 was the first Mercedes-Benz to use the massive 6.3- liter V-8 that produced 250 horsepower. That was definitely needed to push the 5500 to 6000 pound cars (much more when armor plating was added for heads of state) along. And it did the job quite well, up to 130 mph for the "short" 600 four-door limousine. Some of the "hi-tech" luxury items included a central hydraulic system run off the engine that powered everything from the windows and chauffeur's partition to seats, doors, hood and trunk. Other features included self-leveling air-bag suspension, adjustable shock absorbers, powered disc brakes, adjustable steering wheel, dual climate control systems and more.

300SEL 6.3

This is a muscle car in the true sense of the definition. Here Mercedes-Benz stuffed the huge fuel-injected 6333 cc V-8 from the "Grosser" 600 sedan into the smaller, at least relatively, 300SEL sedan's body shell. With 250 horsepower and 369 ft-lbs of torque (for comparison, the awesome ZR-1 Corvette produces 370 ft-lbs of torque), the two-ton sedan could reach a top speed of 140 mph and turn in 0-60 mph times of 6.5 seconds. It was billed, and quite honestly, as the "fastest four-door sedan in the world."

As expected of any Mercedes-Benz luxury sedan, it was fitted with all the luxury amenities like leather upholstery, AM/FM radio, central locking and an air suspension system with self leveling. Most all of the 6,526 300SEL 6.3s built between 1968 and 1972 were equipped with a four-speed automatic transmission, though a few sold in Europe used a four-speed manual. Incidentally, it is estimated that 1,840 were officially imported into the United States. This muscle car is a real sleeper, since the only thing that distinguishes the 300SEL 6.3 from an "ordinary" 300SEL sedan is the discreet "6.3" tag on the trunk lid.

450SEL 6.9

The 450SEL 6.9 continued the high-performance tradition of the 300SEL 6.3. This time, an enlarged (now 6834 cc) version of Mercedes-Benz's biggest V-8 that still produced 250 horsepower in versions sold in the US was used in the new S-class four-door sedan body that was introduced in 1973. What horsepower Mercedes-Benz added, EPA emission requirements and added weight took away. So, while top speed was still at the 140 mph mark, it took a few more seconds to accelerate from 0 to 60 mph. Some 7,380 450SEL 6.9s were produced between 1975 and 1980, with 1816 coming to the US officially. Again, the "6.9" emblem on the trunk was the only visible indication that this was a real "autobahnsturmer."

CONVERTIBLES AND COUPES

300S/Sc

The 300S/Sc that came in coupe, convertible (with rollup windows) and roadster (without roll up windows) form was derived from the contemporary 300 four-door sedans. Compared to the 300 four-door sedans, these grand touring cars were nine inches shorter (195 versus 186 inches) and rode on a 6- inch shorter wheelbase (120 versus 114 inches). The styling was definitely more 1930s than 1950s, and, therefore, these cars are true classics by anyone's definition.

Mercedes-Benz tweaked the 3.0 liter SOHC engine to produce 150 horsepower in the "S" version and 220 horsepower in the mechanically fuel injected "Sc" versions. This was essentially a mildly detuned version of the engine used in the contemporary 300SL. A total of only 560 300S and 200 300Sc were produced between 1952 to 1958 and this includes both coupe and open top models. The sleekest model is the roadster, since the top disappears almost completely, compared to the convertible top complete with landau irons, which leaves the typical German convertible top bustle visible when lowered.

220 Coupe and Convertible

The 220 was Mercedes-Benz's mid-range car through the early 1960s. While most of these 6-cylinder cars were rather mundane but decent performing four-door sedans, Mercedes-Benz also offered cabriolet and coupe versions. Between 1951 and 1955, they used styling that harked back to the 1930s. They even had suicide doors and running boards, and looked like junior versions of the 300S/300Sc. Besides the two passenger (plus jumpseat) convertible, there was a rarer five-passenger convertible as well. While the styling was old, under the hood there was a rather modern chain-driven SOHC engine that produced 80 horsepower.

220S/220SE Convertible and Coupe

The 220 series was updated with a completely new unit construction body design that debuted in 1956. Besides the sedan, there was a 220S cabriolet and 220S coupe. The styling of these special models was a bit more, not a lot more, pleasing than the slab-sided sedans from which they were derived. Initially, the 2-liter SOHC 6-cylinder from the previous 220 equipped with dual Solex carburetors so it produced 85 horsepower was used. After two years of production, the engine was converted to Bosch fuel injection, horsepower went up to 110, and the model was appropriately redesignated the 220SE.

220SEb/250SE/280SE/300SE/280SE 3.5

Like the SLs and SLCs, this series is another example of how Mercedes-Benz creates a variety of models with quite different characters with different engines in the same basic body. This technique can extend the life of a given design without having to re-invest in new tooling.

This series started with the 220SEb that ran between 1960 and 1965. Unlike the contemporary 220S sedans which were introduced a few years earlier and featured "Rambler-like" tailfins, the 220SEbs had a much more pleasing rear-end treatment. As we will see, the styling would endure well beyond the 220SEb and would also evolve into the "S" class sedans that were offered between 1965 and 1972 with a variety of different engines, including a very big V-8 in the 300SEL 6.3. For the 200SEb, the 2195 cc SOHC six-cylinder fuel-injected engine produced 120-134 horsepower. Between 1965 and 1972, the 2.2-liter engine was successively bored out to 2.3, 2.5 and 2.8 liters for the 230SE, 250SE and 280SE versions respectively. These cars varied little in external appearance.

Mercedes-Benz 280SE 3.5   *MBNA Photo*

When it was time to replace the classic 300Sc coupe, roadster and convertible in 1962, the replacement was based on the 220Seb. Power came from the 3.0-liter SOHC, fuel-injected engine used in the 300Sc and 300SL. This top-of-line model was in production through 1967 and featured air suspension. The ultimate car in this series has to be the 280SE 3.5 that appeared in 1969 and was available through 1971. Here, Mercedes-Benz's first generation 3.5-liter overhead cam V-8 was installed in a modified 220SEb-type body to a produce a pretty potent piece of machinery. Unlike previous mechanical fuel injection systems used in Mercedes-Benz, the 3.5-liter used Bosch electronic FI. Only 4,502 280SE 3.5s were produced between 1969 and 1971.

Mercedes-Benzes for Driving and Investing

Virtually every postwar Mercedes-Benz is quite capable of being your only car. There isn't a "fragile" car in the bunch. Of course, you wouldn't want to commute to work in a car like a 300SL gullwing or a 300Sc roadster, not because they aren't up to the task, but they are just too valuable. In all fairness, it's because they are based on decades-old technology, 50s and early 60s models are also a bit cumbersome to handle. However, cars like the later model SL roadsters, SLC coupes, post 220SEb coupes and cabriolets, 300SEL 6.3s and 450SEL 6.9s are equal to, or indeed can surpass, just about any 1990s car in all categories - performance, handling, reliability, durability, creature comforts - everything but fuel economy. All these high-performance Benzs are quite thirsty. And there is the matter of image. Even a decade-old, but well-cared-for Mercedes-Benz of just about any model still carries more "image" than the latest Lexus or Infiniti. - sort of like "old" versus "new" money.

The adage "buy the best and ignore the rest" goes double for collectible Mercedes-Benz models. While the cars discussed here epitomize Mercedes-Benz quality and durability, a worn-out Mercedes-Benz can be very costly to maintain and repair, let alone restore. And there are many latter-day models that have seen service as daily drivers, often as business transportation, frequently under lease, and may have had several previous owners. High performance cars are usually bought by high performance drivers, so many of these have seen hard miles, not a problem if it didn't involve outright abuse and lack of proper maintenance.

Also, high mileage is not a real detriment (Mercedes-Benz are designed to go hundreds of thousands of miles) if the car was well maintained. Do not be afraid of an exceptionally well-maintained Mercedes-Benz with 100,000 or more miles on the odometer, but make sure that the maintenance is documented in detail. When you start shopping for a Mercedes-Benz, you will be pleasantly surprised by the large number of owners who have complete service records to show you. Indeed, a complete set of records can actually increase the value of an individual car, or least be a great selling point.

While repairs on a Mercedes-Benz may not be frequent, parts and labor can be quite costly. Parts, especially mechanical ones, are readily available. Mercedes-Benz itself stocks many parts for vintage models, and, surprisingly, their prices are often quite competitive with other sources of parts. Because Mercedes-Benz uses mechanical componentry for long production runs and in many different models, knowledge about part interchangeability takes on an important role in maintaining or restoring a Mercedes-Benz. Many a lesser Mercedes-Benz sedan has become a donor vehicle for a more valuable coupe or roadster. Specialized body parts and trim especially for low production models can be a different story.

Because many of the higher performance models were not officially imported by Mercedes-Benz of North America, most of these more desirable models were brought in as "gray market" cars. Thus, they are often seen in the "for sale" columns. As with any gray market purchase, make sure all the car's papers are in order before you sign the check. Also, more than one purchaser has been burned by buying a car sight unseen from Europe with a fresh coat of paint that is actually a rusted and worn-out car. Finally, these might be European models without air-conditioning, leather interiors, power windows, etc. In the US, these are items expected on top-of-line Benzes, so such a car might be more difficult to resell. Also, Europe-only cars may contain mechanical components or trim that might prove hard to replace in the US.

The Mercedes-Benz 300SL gullwing coupe has been one of the most spectacular automotive investments, not just among Mercedes-Benz models. In the early 70s, they were still selling for around $5,000. Now, pristine examples have sold for 100 times more. Will prices climb more? Perhaps, not on this scale, but then again Mercedes-Benz isn't creating any new ones. Later model SLs are appreciating, even though there are lots of them around. Recent model SLs will probably at least retain their current values. When people look at sticker prices on the latest 300SL and 500SL, they might be in the market for an earlier SL. These offer almost everything found on the latest models except the mega-buck prices. This may also happen with later model "S" class sedans which were not discussed here. Incidentally, if you want much of the looks and character of an SL at a lower price, you might look at a SLC coupe, which might be necessary if you need rear seat capacity. Of course, the top doesn't come down.

How To Get Started In Mercedes-Benz

The preface to successfully buying and owning a collectible Mercedes-Benz should be a membership in the Mercedes-Benz Club of America. You'll find them at 1907 Lelaray Street, Colorado Springs, CO 80909 719-633-6427. The club publishes the bimonthly magazine <u>The Star</u>, which contains informative articles and advertising for goods and services helpful to the collector. The club also has nearly 100 regional representatives located throughout all the states and Canada who will assist you in your Mercedes-Benz-related activities.

About The Author

Bill Siuru is a retired USAF Colonel who is now a writer on aviation and automotive subjects. Growing up in Detroit, he was side-tracked from his primary interest in cars by a 24-year career in Air Force R & D. With a doctorate in mechanical engineering, Bill has taught engineering at both West Point and the USAF Academy. He has been a German car enthusiast since the mid-seventies, when he bought his first Mercedes-Benz, an "S" sedan. He has written eight books and over 1,000 articles for such publications as the BMW <u>Roundel</u>, <u>Autoweek</u>, <u>Car Collector</u>, <u>Special Interest Autos</u> and others.

YEAR	LINE	Relative Condition: Worse ↔ Better		
		❸	❷	❶
1952—1955	300S Coupe	70000	95000	120000
1952—1955	300S Cabriolet	135000	170000	200000
1956—1958	300SC Coupe	115000	140000	165000
1956—1958	300SC Cabriolet	320000	390000	470000
1955—1963	190SL Roadster	17000	22000	29000
1957—1963	300SL Roadster	190000	220000	255000
1955—1957	300SL Gullwing	220000	265000	320000
1957—1959	220S Coupe	11000	17500	23500
1956—1959	220S Cabriolet	23000	29000	38000
1958—1960	220SE Coupe	11500	17500	24000
1958—1960	220SE Cabriolet	23000	30000	39000
1963—1968	230SL Roadster	12500	17500	25000
1966—1968	250SL Roadster	12500	17500	26000
1968—1971	280SL Roadster	13500	20000	29000
1960—1965	220S/SE Coupe	6500	11000	16500

YEAR	LINE	Relative Condition: Worse ↔ Better		
		❸	❷	❶
1961—1965	220S/SE Cabriolet	20000	30000	37000
1965—1967	250S/SE Coupe	7500	12000	18500
1965—1967	250S/SE Cabriolet	21000	31000	39000
1965—1967	300SE Coupe	8500	13000	19000
1962—1967	300SE Cabriolet	26000	37000	46000
1968—1972	280SE Coupe	9500	13500	19000
1968—1972	280SE Cabriolet	26000	35000	45000
1970—1971	280SE 3.5 Coupe	11500	15500	24000
1970—1971	280SE 3.5 Cabriolet	46000	57000	76000
1968—1972	300SEL 6.3 Sedan	9000	13500	20000
1969—1972	250C/CE Coupe	4000	6000	8000
1972—1980	450SL Roadster	12000	18000	23000
1973—1980	450SL C Coupe	8500	13000	17000
1977—1979	450SEL 6.9 Sedan	11000	15500	23000 .
1978—1981	280CE Coupe	6000	9000	13500

MG

BY BILL HARKINS

THE AURA OF THE OCTAGON

Whenever an MG appears at a car event, someone inevitably says, "I had one just like that in college", or "My father had an MG when I was a kid". For over 68 years, the famous octagon has symbolized the spirit of MG. What began in the twenties as a modest little company in Abingdon, England, became one of the most intense groups of creative automobile designers and builders in the world, with an ardent following on all continents. In fact, MG ownership has a virtual cult aspect in the US, England, Australia, Canada and New Zealand.

There's a network of clubs, MG regalia treasured by members in their "MG rooms", registers of specific models and a worldwide specialist industry in manufacture of new parts to keep them running. MG car meets can be found almost every weekend, and large regional meetings of owners of the older models in the US are called "Gathering of the Faithful". MGs were designed to be practical and economical to buy and maintain and are, relatively, still inexpensive in the exotic arena of collector cars. For the new collector of import cars, MGs deserve attention for fun, performance, and driveability at reasonable prices.

MG HISTORY

The MG story began in 1921 when William Morris, the British automobile magnate, hired young Cecil Kimber as General Manager for Morris Garages, a car service business in Oxford run independently of the Morris car factory. Kimber was more than a repair shop manager. He was creative, ambitious and fervently interested in cars. He began modifying Mr. Morris' chassis for increased performance, and built his first competition sports car, now referred to as "Old Number One", in 1925. He was soon selling modified Morris cars under the name MG, the initials of the garage business. The famous octagon logo appeared around 1927.

The initial successes of Kimber's early sports cars led to the design of a totally new chassis called the Midget, based on the new Morris Minor 847cc overhead-camshaft four-cylinder engine. This baby car of the day became known as the M-type and in 1929 was the first real MG sports car produced. From a new factory at Abingdon, a steady stream of new and improved models of MGs was created and built for enthusiasts around the world for the succeeding 51 years.

To describe the alphabet soup of MG models produced in the thirties (Cs, Ds, Fs, Js, Ks, Ls, Ps) is not possible in this chapter. For six years the factory produced a stream of successful competition four and six-cylinder, single-overhead-cam-engined machines that won virtually hundreds of races, rallies and hillclimbs in England and Europe. The famous supercharged K3, of which only 33 were built, was one of the most fabulous race cars of all time. Today, these cars rarely change hands; but if they do, they fetch up to a half million dollars!

This discussion of collectible MGs will not cover such exotica, but will present the practical postwar MGs that you can readily buy today, which have evolved from a very distinguished heritage.

In 1935, MG discontinued factory-sponsored racing and the ohc cars were discontinued. A new line of midget sports cars was produced using conventional pushrod engines of 1292 cc displacement, designated the TA model. An improved engine was developed for the car in 1939, known as the TB, which is rare today, as only 379 were produced due to the outbreak of World War II.

Although some restored models sell for prices in excess of $100,000, lower-priced prewar MGs that you can acquire for less money usually will require full restoration, long searches for scarce parts, and often take several years to complete. The prewar T-series MG was the predecessor of the famous postwar MG TC, the first one exported to America.

THE POSTWAR T-TYPE MG

After the war, Britain focused on rebuilding its industrial base and the government urged the export of cars. MG had exported only to Europe, but American GIs in England discovered the MG and it was love at first sight. The post-war MG was a slightly modified TB and the factory converted from wartime tank and aircraft production to sports cars late in 1945. Only 100 new cars were completed.

The freshman collector should understand that the T-type MGs, so popular in the fifties, are not efficient for regular driving today. The obsolete engineering of the wood-framed bodies, low horsepower, and minimal interior space are not compatible with today's traffic. They are however, the pride and joy of T-club members who travel in caravans of great camaraderie with their pampered and coddled vintage MGs.

TC Classic Lines

The most outstanding attribute of the TC, and the main reason to own one, is the graceful proportion of its classic design, which has remained attractive for over 45 years. In 1950, the New York Museum of Modern Art held an exhibit called "Eight Automobiles" and the MG TC was included. Although available only with right-hand drive, almost all of the 10,000 TCs produced came to America. The ride was hard as a rock, the steering vague, and even in the late forties it was quite underpowered with its 54hp engine. None of these shortcomings prevented hundreds of enthusiasts from driving them as hard as they would go in races over ordinary roads, usually the more winding, the better. America's only World Champion race driver, Phil Hill, began his career in a TC.

MG-TC   *Richard Knudson Photo*

Today, TCs are scarce, very desirable, and are priced in the $25,000 to $35,000 range when in top condition. Non-runners or worn out specimens sell for less, but the search for parts can be formidable for the first time MG collector.

The TD-designed for America

The MG design staff recognized the need to offer a more modern car for export. In 1950, the TD was introduced; a new chassis, front coil spring suspension, smooth rack and pinion steering and, of course, left-hand drive for those markets that drive that way. Gone were the wire wheels and, to many previous MG owners, the ambience of the classic TC style. Almost 30,000 TDs were produced, and most of them were exported to America. The TD was also used actively in sports car racing and it bred numerous "specials" in order to go faster. Abingdon responded to the quest for more power from American buyers and delivered the Mark II, with extra shocks, dual fuel pumps and 1.5 inch carburetors. Unfortunately, these changes produced less than three additional horsepower.

TDs and their parts are relatively plentiful and this model has shown some, but not spectacular, appreciation in recent years. Mark IIs tend to demand an unrealistic premium due to the low production of only 1022 units. If you are interested in a Mark II, be aware that one can be simulated by adding the extra parts. The genuine article, however, had the engine number prefix of TD/c, an air cleaner bulge on the right-hand hood panel, and the extra shock absorber mountings are not easily faked.

MG-TD   *Richard Knudson Photo*

The TF-the In-Between Model

In 1953, MG brought out another evolution of the T-type. Abingdon had realized the comparative stodginess of the TD in the postwar world and had a truly new model on the drawing boards. Design was stalled due to the priority of introducing the Austin-Healey 100, a product of British Motors Corporation, which now owned MG. Abingdon knew they had to do something to bolster the TD's diminishing sales, and the TF was concocted by a small design group in just a few weeks. It was a valid effort to hold American sales for three years, but only 9600 TFs were produced.

Historically, it has been a habit of MG aficionados to impugn the latest model. The TF, with its molded fender headlamps, octagonally-shaped instruments, and the heretical slanted radiator grille with a fake cap, caused an uproar among the purists. Today, however, the car is considered by some to be the best of the T-series. Fully restored specimens are not quite at the price level of TCs, but asking prices are often in the low to mid $20,000 range.

In the continuing quest for more power, the TF 1500 version was offered, which had a slightly larger engine of 1466cc. The result was worth another 6 hp, raising it from 57 to 63 hp. Only 3600 were built, so it carries the scarcity premium. Because of its low production, it is now highly prized, but parts are getting scarce. If you seek the charm of a vintage MG with relative driving ease, scarcity as a collectible and a steady appreciation, the TF 1500 is worth investigation.

WRITER'S CHOICE

Say you have a $25,000 budget and want a condition 1 vehicle. Writer's choice is between the TC and the TF. The TC will continue to gain in value as a classic style, historic automobile. This author is convinced that one day the prestigious Classic Car Club of America will accept the TC into its ranks along side the prewar MG K3 and SA models.

The TF provides similar rarity but possesses the capability of being driven comfortably at posted speed limits. The decision becomes one of patience in locating the vehicle and deciding how you wish to drive it.

The MGA- A Modern MG

A completely new MG was needed to meet increasing competition and the MG technical staff realized in the early 50's that better aerodynamics would be required. The new design incorporated major components of the BMC line to take economic advantage of volume production which had been the operating style of MG since Kimber's days. MG traditionally introduced new models to the public by means of an initial racing success. This was true of the slick new design which roared on to the world sports car scene in 1955 at the 24-hour race of Le Mans, France. Three prototypes were entered, and two finished 5th and 6th in their class behind three Porsches-a formidable achievement.

MG began the alphabet again and called the new car the MGA. At the famous Montlhery track in France, five MGAs ran 100 miles in an hour. The sports car market recognized that MG had finally done something new, and boldly the motoring press extolled a winner. The frame was wider to allow low seating between the rails, and a tooled steel body featured distinctly contemporary styling. It was a great performer, and for many years enjoyed competition success in its class in England, Europe and America. The strong attraction to the MGA by the American market resulted in almost two-thirds of the total production coming to the US.

Despite the initial success, there were some practical short-comings in the design. It was still not possible to lock an MGA for the protection of valuables, for example. Another holdover from the Ts were side curtains rather than windup windows. The two 6-volt batteries located behind the seats were difficult to access. These deficiencies were not of concern to the US market, which was more interested in performance, handling, appearance and a reasonable price. The MGA sold for about $2200. Under the hood was a decently powered engine of 1492cc producing 68 hp in the 5000rpm range. A very satisfying 85 mph was attainable in the MGA 1500 offered in roadster form. In October 1956, a coupe appeared that improved some of the roadster's faults. The doors could be locked, the windows rolled up and an honest 100+ mph achieved. The MGA 1500 was so successful that its production of 58,750 exceeded all previous post-war models.

MGA Twin-Cam

Recognizing a good product in the MGA, Abingdon was at work developing enhanced versions to continue the MG tradition of improving the breed. Experimentation with a twin-cam engine had been in progress during MGA development, and in 1958 it was introduced to the market. Output became 107hp at 6500 rpm with an increased displacement of 1588cc to compete in the 1600cc sports car racing class. With disc brakes all around and center-lock disc wheels, this was truly a hot MG. It boasted a top speed of 120 mph and was reasonably priced at $3345.

Despite the improvements, the twin-cam was not fully competitive when racing against such cars as the Austin Healey 100. With an initial compression ratio of 9.9:1, it required higher octane fuel than was generally available. Ignition timing and engine maintenance were critical, and with the difficulty of engine access due to the small hood opening, service was often neglected. Other problems were possible damage to the engine by over-revving and the chrome piston rings were a cause of high oil consumption.

MGA Twin Cams   *Richard Knudson Photo*

Due to fussy tuning and upkeep, the twin-cam was not a suitable road machine for the average buyer, and production was discontinued in April 1960 with a total of only 2111 units. Today the "Twinkie" is very rare and concours models sell in the $40-45,000 range. Parts are exceedingly scarce, usually requiring a world-wide search, and with the critical tuning needed to develop its full potential, it is probably not the model for the neophyte car collector.

The MGA 1600/1600 Mark II

In an effort to increase performance without the fussiness of the twin-cam design, the MGA 1600 was introduced in May of 1959. The earlier push-rod engine was increased to the same displacement as the twin-cam, 1588cc, giving 80hp. This was a successful upgrade in the market with a total production of 31,501 cars. You can identify a 1600 model immediately by its separate brake and tail light configuration

In 1961, a further upgrade of the engine was introduced as the MGA 1600 Mark II, when its displacement was raised to 1622cc, which produced 93hp. But, the model was nearing the end of its market life and only 8719 units were produced. Appearance changes were minuscule, most noticeably, the revised radiator grille with its almost vertical slats, and horizontal tail lights set below the trunk lid. An even rarer version was created when twin-cam production ended, with 389 sets of four-wheel disc brakes and chassis left over that were mated with the 1600 pushrod engine and designated the MGA 1600 Mark II De Luxe. This is the rarest MGA of all, and may eventually exceed the twin-cam in value.

Despite that MGA's overall success, after seven years, the market was ready for an improved MG, and in early 1962 the last MGA rolled off the line. Total volume was 101,181, again exceeding production of all prior postwar MGs.

WRITER'S CHOICE

For the beginning MG car collector interested in the MGA, the 1600 or 1600 Mk II is preferred. These models combine driveability and handling with the additional power for modern highway travel plus the potential of better appreciation due to scarcity. Specimens of these models in excellent condition can be located at $8-10,000. Parts are readily available, and maintenance can be accomplished by the average enthusiast. Appreciation potential is good, as the MGA is gaining in popularity for collectors due to the scarcity and relative impracticality of the T-series.

The Unitized Body MGs

Throughout the life of the MGA many factory and dealer accessories were offered, which was indicative of the changing sports car market. Buyers wanted family-car amenities with sports-car performance. Abingdon clearly recognized that the inconveniences of the fifties would no longer be acceptable, and the next MG was a fully contemporary design for the times. MG had finally gotten their act together and produced, for over 18 years, what was the world's most successful sports car.

The MGB

The new design, the MGB, used a monocoque body shell, very stiff and strong, into which was mounted the BMC B-series 3-main-bearing engine bored to 1798cc and producing 94hp. Body lines, influenced by one of MG's numerous speed-record-breaking special designs, and with some assistance by Pininfarina of Turin, Italy, became one of the best-looking two-seaters ever produced. Almost 30 years after its introduction, it is still a clean, modern design. Initially, independent rear suspension had been considered but was dropped, as it was felt that the additional cost would not provide significant improvement. Today, with its solid rear axle, the MGB will still out-corner TRs and E-type Jaguars.

MGB   *MG Photo*

The MGB, like its predecessor, was successful due to the designers' assiduous use of high-volume BMC components. The introduction date of September 1962 was followed by many improvements for several years, including overdrive in 1963, and five main bearings in the GT hardtop model in 1965. The GT was extremely successful for poor weather areas and was bought by people who would never have considered an open sports car. With styling assistance again by Pininfarina, the GT was one of the first "hatchbacks", an innovation now commonplace in world car design. Although slightly heavier (160 pounds) than the roadster, it was a bit faster because of improved aerodynamics. In 1968, a fully-synchromesh gearbox and an alternator were incorporated, and the model became the Mk II. Automatic transmission (no kidding!) was also available, but not surprisingly, there were few buyers and it was eventually withdrawn.

1967 is considered by many to be the watershed for the MGB and the company, although production went on for another 12 years and an additional 375,000 units. From 1968, MG was beset with safety and emission control regulations which eventually lead to the termination of the car and the company. Whereas the initial announcement of the MGB had been greeted so enthusiastically by the motoring press, changes from 1969 were harshly criticized. With the problems of the US and European regulations and the internecine management turmoil within British Leyland who had absorbed BMC, MG also faced formidable competition from the Japanese, notably the Datsun 240Z coupe.

MGB GT   *MG Photo*

The 1969 -1973 models, even with their power-sapping smog pump and safety-related body changes still enjoyed a healthy US market. From 1974 until the last unit rolled off the line in 1980, cars for export to the states were more affected by government regulation than car design principles. Ride height was raised 1 1/2 inches, massive crash bumpers were installed, a single Zenith carburetor was fed strangled air and, with a catalytic converter, horsepower was reduced from 95 to 70, slightly more than the original MGA.

It would appear at present that there is a strong MG market for which no manufacturer exists. This is indicated by the offering of the British Motor Heritage Organization (a division of Rover Cars which absorbed Leyland) which authorizes small manufacturers to reproduce parts for certain out-of-production cars. The entire MGB body tooling has been refurbished, and a new body shell is now available to MGB owners for building virtually a brand new car. These are available from major MG parts dealers in the US at about $4000. This leads to the conclusion that the MGB will be with us well into the next century.

The Rare MGC and MGB GT V8

In the constant quest by MG for improved performance, the design staff developed a six-cylinder model which was introduced in September 1967 as the MGC. With a 150hp, 2912cc engine, and torsion bar front suspension, it was expected to perform well in 3-liter class competition. Unfortunately, the additional 400 pounds created poor weight distribution which caused handling problems. It was fast, however, up to 124 mph with overdrive.

MGC   *MG Photo*

The motoring press was not enthusiastic. Acceleration was poor at low speeds and only the hood bulge to clear the carburetors distinguished the new car from the MGB. Sales were not high, and as a result, only 8999 were produced, split about evenly between roadsters and GTs. Manufacture ceased in 1969. In the collector car field, a less-than-satisfactory model during its production life may become, years after it is out of production, a "collectible". This is true of the MGC, which now enjoys its own Register both in England and North America. It is not a beginner's MG, however, as few mechanical parts are interchangeable with the MGB and they are very scarce. However, prices have not skyrocketed and top condition MGCs could become considerably more valuable than MGBs over the next few years.

The last development effort at Abingdon was the MGB GT V8 introduced in 1972, and what might have been MG's best car. The Rover 3-liter engine was supplied and fitted to the MG GT with minimal body modification. Production was limited to right-hand drive, so no exports were made to the US. Only 2591 were produced and production ended in 1976 thus creating another rare MG. Recently, conversion kits have been offered in the US allowing the current Rover V8 to be installed in the MGB roadster. Such a conversion, like other engine swapping efforts, does not create a better car for the collector. In addition, there is the problem of obtaining proper emission control to pass smog tests. The V8 MG or its conversion kits are not recommended for the apprentice MG collector.

The New MG Midget

By 1966, MG was second to VW in total sales of imported cars in America. Part of this success was due to the other monocoque bodied model, the post-war Midget. The new Midget was produced a year earlier than the MGB as an outgrowth of Austin-Healey's small sports car, the Sprite. With its oddly protruding headlights, the Sprite immediately became known as the "bug-eye". MG introduced their version in May 1961, directed toward the market once covered by the T-Series. This was another MG success with over 250,000 produced through 1979, more than double the MGA volume.

Midget models evolved into three separate Marks: I, 948cc and 1098cc; II, 1098cc; III, 1275cc and 1493cc. The initial engine was too small for the modern market and was quickly enlarged to produce 55hp, more than the early Ts. In 1964, the Mk II provided improved suspension and rollup windows. The 1965 Mk III increased horsepower to 65 with the use of the Mini-Cooper engine, a very successful engine in British sedan racing and rallies.

The Midget was in direct competition with the Triumph Spitfire, and in 1974 the final evolution of the Mk III Midget incorporated the 1500cc Spitfire engine. The Mk III could attain 100mph, was less expensive than its larger MGB brother, yet offered considerable comfort for the 70s despite its rather small, cramped cockpit for six-footers.

The Leyland decade of 1968-1978 was a ponderous, bureaucratic era for MG and, after much turmoil, production of the marque ceased in 1980 and the Abingdon factory was closed. One of the great chapters of automotive history had ended leaving a huge world-wide following of enthusiasts who continue to enjoy their highly collectible MGs.

WRITER'S CHOICE

For the initial import car collector, an MG Midget is a good start. Parts are still readily available, and it is highway driveable at a reasonable price. A decent late-model Midget will range from $3000 to $5500. Unfortunately, despite the original high production and current low price, good rust-free Midgets are not easily found. The Mk III is recommended for the higher power required for today's traffic conditions.

In summer of 1991, the Heritage Organization announced the availability of a complete Midget body shell, made to original specifications from resurrected factory tooling. This demonstrates the newly found British determination to keep the Midgets and MGBs running, and should be considered by any import car collector as a factor in selecting a particular marque. Who else is reproducing completely new body shells?

As for MGBs, the ideal choice is the 1966 or 1967 roadster with the overdrive and wire wheel option. The power is not dragged down by smog equipment, and the chrome bumpers are much better looking than the later model rubber safety components. For less than $10,000, a condition 1 car can be located and this represents the best value in a collectable sports car today. By 1992, the car will be considered an "antique" and qualify for low-cost limited-mileage antique car insurance, yet still be freeway comfortable. In addition, the mechanically inclined enthusiast can perform his own maintenance to preserve the value.

MGs TO AVOID

While some models of MGs were not successful in their production period, it is also true that some models were quite successful in certain markets during production, but are not as desirable now as collector cars. In general, this is true of the postwar MG sedans. During the 1950s and 1960s, MG produced several sedan models such as the Y-series, the ZA and ZB series Magnettes, and the 1100 and 1300cc cars. These products had considerable success in England, but were not greeted with enthusiasm by the American market. The early MG sedans have little collector demand, meager appreciation and should be avoided at this time.

One exception is the MG YT four-passenger open tourer which is quite rare, as only 877 were built, but it is probably not for the beginning MG collector. The other MGs to avoid now as collector cars are the post-1974 MGBs. If one is looking for a low-priced two-seater sports car without concern for overall performance, these MGs are quite plentiful in the market, but will not appreciate to the extent of the earlier models.

ACQUIRING AN MG

The first question of the beginning MG student is how to locate a suitable car. One of the standard markets for rare and exotic collector cars are the numerous auctions held throughout the country. While these are entertaining events, MGs are not commonly offered for sale. A proper evaluation of the car's condition cannot be made on the auction lot nor can they be driven. Go to auctions for fun, but not to buy MGs.

Another source is the periodicals that cater to the old car market. One of the best known is Hemmings Motor News. While there will be a selection of Ts, As and Bs each month, they will be scattered throughout the country. A listing of the specific car of your choice and condition may not appear often, and it may be 1500 miles from your home. By the time you call, it could have been sold.

One of the best ways to acquire your MG is to join an MG club at both the national and local level and read the club's newsletters. Not only will you find the cars, but you will meet the people who can help with information, technical assistance and locating scarce parts. A guide to national MG car clubs is included at the end of this chapter. They all have local chapters in major metropolitan areas.

MGBs can still be found in regular used car advertising and the weekly "trader" publications available in many cities. Increasingly, these are limited to the less-desirable late model cars, but an early one will occasionally be listed. Locating a suitable MG can take several months, so be patient.

Buying Guidelines

The first recommendation is to look at several examples of the car you seek. You must develop this discipline because, when you see a desirable car, it will be tempting to make an offer thinking that it will be gone if you don't. At this stage, you are still learning about MGs. Remember, you are not just buying a used car for transportation this is to be your pride and joy, and hopefully will gain in value under your careful maintenance. Since the car will probably be from 15 to 45 years old, a very careful examination is in order. The objective is not to get a lower price (you may not in any case), but to determine what work will be required after purchase to get it in good running order, and to decide if you are willing to take it on with awareness of its condition.

You should bring or have with you: a good flashlight for seeing into dark corners of the chassis, an icepick to check for rotted wood in T-types (and rust in all models), a jack to look under the chassis, a compression gauge, a magnet to detect the presence of plastic body filler, an eyedropper to sample brake fluid, and plenty of rags to wipe off grease and grime from parts of the car and yourself. If at all possible, bring a knowledgeable MG friend as well.

LOOKING FOR THE TIN WORM

Unless you are considering a fresh restoration, which will be priced accordingly, there is likely to be body rust. This is not insurmountable if confined to easily repairable areas, but you will want to know before purchase to what extent rust must be removed and metal replaced. This is going to be compounded in T-types with the potential for rotted wood in the body framing. Take your icepick and poke at the large main member under each door. It should not go into the wood more than 1/8 inch if it is sound. More than 1/8 inch could mean that replacement of the lower sill is required. This and other pieces can be replaced without rebodying the car, but unless you are willing to obtain or build a new body shell, any significant indication of body rot should be avoided. It will be cheaper to buy a restored T-type than to be faced with the need for a new body and idling the car for a year or more.

On MGAs, rust can appear at the inside front of the rear wheel opening and eat into the door frame if no splash shield is present. Another rust point is the floor of the trunk. A replacement floor can be obtained, but installation is not recommended for the do-it-yourselfer. On MGA coupes, rust can form at the joint of the top and body. Rust that has eaten clear through the metal leaving rough, brown edged holes ("lace underwear") will be easily seen and is a signal to walk away.

What is more difficult to detect is beginning rust with the tell-tale sign of slightly bubbling paint over the rusting area. Although the front of the MGA frame will usually be rust-free because of grease and road dirt, the rear corners of the frame can rust and be quite difficult to see without jacking up the car and crawling underneath. Replacement parts are available which can be welded in. However, such a repair will detract from the future value of the car.

On all MGs, expect problems around the battery mountings. On Ts, the bottom of the bulkhead battery box has usually been propped up with wood, or the battery is sitting on two pieces of angle iron. On MGAs and Bs, the twin batteries are at the rear of the chassis, and may have been neglected for years. These are not difficult to repair, however. MGs are often advertised as a "California Car", implying a rust-free condition. Be sure it is not a California **beach** car which can have the combination of moisture and salt, a metallic disaster. If all the chrome is slightly but evenly pitted, consider it a signal of salt-laden air.

MECHANICAL INSPECTION

Start the engine, and using the compression gauge, check for consistent pressure of 120 psi or more in all cylinders. A drop in pressure on one cylinder will indicate the need for some engine work. Shock absorbers can be checked by bouncing each corner of the car. It should stop moving after one or two bounces. Typically, shocks in MGBs wore out easily, but are readily available. Using the eyedropper, examine the brake fluid for black specks which would indicate a breakdown of rubber parts in the master cylinder.

On MGBs, watch for signs of body repair from a significant collision. This will require examination on a lift, so bring along a good body man if necessary. The magnet can be used to spot the improper use of plastic body filler in suspected areas. While the car is up, wiggle the front wheels from top to bottom to check for bearing play and king pin wear in T-types. Then try to turn the driveshaft in gear to see if there is excessive play indicating wear in the universal joints.

Ask the owner if maintenance or repair records are available. If it's a fresh restoration, ask to look at the list of parts purchased or work performed. An absence of documentation, unless you are planning a total restoration, may be an indication of lackadaisical concern for maintenance by the owner.

TEST DRIVING

If things look reasonable at this point, a test drive is in order. Warm up the engine and with the brake pedal depressed and in gear, let out the clutch. The engine should immediately die, otherwise a worn clutch may be indicated. Drive to a steep incline and see if the hand brake will hold the car while in neutral. When on the road, check for brake pull to one side. On a smooth road, move to the center of the road and take your hands off the wheel to see if the steering tracks straight. This will not be possible with a TC, but you don't buy a TC for its steering anyway. Watch for blue smoke out of the exhaust; while accelerating this shows ring wear, while decelerating it shows valve wear.

If you are testing a T-type, drive down a steep hill in 2nd and 3rd gear without using the accelerator to see if it jumps out of gear. This is common on older Ts, but is not a difficult repair from the top of the gearbox. The TC had one of the best gearboxes of all MGs, almost indestructible. By now the oil should be hot, so check the gauge, which should be holding around 40 psi. If it is 20 to 25 psi at road speed, engine work will be needed. Check that the ammeter is showing a charge of 2 to 4 amps. No movement or a negative reading indicates electrical work required. The final test is to check all electrical components, head and tail lights, parking lights, horn, and turn signals. All of these are easily corrected if faulty, but may provide points for negotiation in your favor.

"ALL NUMBERS MATCH"

For the serious collector, this indication in an ad is critical. A true collector car should have the same engine and chassis numbers with which it left the factory. There are many sources for determining number sequences for the various MG models, often in parts dealer's catalogs. If you are looking at an expensive T-type, do not accept only the brass ID plate as the final word, since they are available new and can be renumbered. Look at the left front frame rail where the stamped chassis number will be found. The owner will know you are serious and knowledgeable.

With MGBs there have been various engine swaps and modifications over the years. The matching number issue may not be as critical to the MGB buyer who is interested in the car for use as a daily driver. However, in the case of an older, more expensive MG, the numbers can be critical for eventual resale or, if a fresh restoration, for high point judging in competitive showing.

Lastly, have at hand a few of the many excellent books available on your MG of choice, as well as the appropriate shop manual. These can be of great value in evaluating the claims of an owner about his priceless MG. In fact, collecting MG books and literature can be rewarding, as scarce pre-war titles have a world-wide market!

THE LONG-TERM VIEWPOINT

The future of MG collecting appears very bright. World-wide enthusiasm appears to be higher today than during the marque's manufacture. There are constant rumors out of Rover of a brand new MG, and a sleek futuristic prototype has been seen at auto shows. Whether a new MG ever appears, the value of existing MGs is assured.

There has been a tendency in the US for MG groups to partition themselves into T, A or B clubs as if they were separate marques. This is not true in other countries, where MG meets will have the full range of models on hand from prewar to late MGB's. As T owners retire and sell off their cars over the next 10 or 15 years, it is quite likely that the buyers will be MG enthusiasts who bought their MGAs or Bs today and would like to own a representative model of the earlier era while still enjoying their "vintage" 1960s era MG on the highway.

You are now ready to join the thousands of international enthusiasts who have discovered the Aura of the Octagon-the MG.

MG PARTS/CLUBS LISTING

Parts and Service Sources

Moss Motors, Ltd.
7200 Hollister Avenue
Box 847
Goleta CA 92116
Phone: 800-235-6954
Fax: 805-968-6910
(T/A/B/Midget parts)

Abingdon Spares, Ltd.
Box 37
South Street
Walpole, NH 03608
Phone: 800-225-9251
Fax: 603-756-9614
(T-series parts)

Victoria British, Ltd.
Box 14991
Lenexa, Kansas 66215
Phone: 800-255-0088
Fax: 913-599-3299
(A/B/Midget parts)

Commonwealth Classic Cars
496 North Coast Highway
Laguna Beach, CA 92651
Phone: 714-494-8172
Fax: 714-497-2221
(T-series, new and used parts)

NTG Motor Services, Ltd.
21 St. Margaret's Green
Ipswich 1P4 2BN
England
04730211240
(T-series parts)

Naylor Brothers, Ltd.
Regent House, Dockfield Road
Shipley, West Yorkshire BD17 7SF
England
Phone 0274-594071
(T-series parts, wood body frames)

Sports & Vintage Motors, Ltd.
Upper Battlefield
Shrewsbury SY4 3DB
England
Phone: 0930-210458
Fax: 0939-210644
(Early T-series parts)

Pre-war MG Parts Centre
1A Albany Road
Chislehurst, Kent BR7 6BG
England
Phone: 081-467-7788
Fax: 081-295-1277
(Scarce Pre-war and T-series parts)

Barry Bone
Quions, Jarvis Lane
Steyning, West Sussex BN44 3GA
England
Phone: 0903-813355
Fax: 0403-864864
(Scarce, used T-series parts)

Whitworth Shop
14444 Watt Road
Novelty, OH 44072
Phone: 216-338-5950
(T-series instruments, body tubs)

White Post Restorations
White Post, VA 22663
Phone: 703-837-1140
(T-series brake cylinder resleeving)

University Motors Ltd.
614 Eastern Avenue SE
Grand Rapids, MI 49503
Phone: 616-245-2141
Fax: 616-245-MGMG
(T/A/B parts, service, tech seminars)

Vintage Restorations
The Old Bakery
Windmill Street
Tunbridge Wells
Kent TN2 4UU
England
(Instrument restoration)

A. W. Bell Australia Pty. Ltd.
4-6 King Street
Oakley, Victoria
Australia, 3166
Phone: 03-568-4622
(T-series tools)

British Auto Electric
2722 East Carnival Ave.
Anaheim, CA 92806
Phone: 714-630-1074
(Electrical repair/restoration, all models)

Auto Vintagery
7757 Girard Avenue
La Jolla, CA 92037
Phone: 619-459-0805
(MGA twin cam parts)

Special Interest Car Parts
1340 Hartford Avenue
Johnston, RI 02919
Phone: 410-831-8850
(MGB parts)

Scarborough Faire
1151 Main Street
Pawtucket, RI 02865
Phone: 410-724-4200
Fax: 410-724-5392
(MGA parts)

O'Conner Classic Autos
2569 Scott Boulevard
Santa Clara, CA 95050
Phone: 408-727-0430
(T-series engine rebuilding)

Rhode Island Wiring Service
Box 434H
West Kingston, RI 02892
Phone: 401-789-1955
(Wiring harnesses, all models)

Lewis Restoration Products
Box 127
Lompoc, CA 93438
Phone: 805-736-5089
(British nuts/bolts/taps/dies)

MG CAR CLUBS - US AND UK

National level MG Car Club Ltd.
Kimber House
Box 251
Abingdon, Oxon. OX14 1FF
England
Phone: 0235-555552
One of the oldest car clubs in the world, founded in 1930. Has Registers for all MG models.

New England MG T—Register
Drawer 220 Oneonta, NY 13820
Phone: 607-432-6835
For T-series owners, national club, publishes The Sacred Octagon bimonthly.

Octagon Car Club
36 Queensville Ave
Stafford ST17 4LS
England
Phone: 785-51014
For pre-1956 MG owners, offers parts at discount to members, monthly journal.

American MGB Association
PO Box 11401
Chicago, IL 60611
Phone: 312-437-3897
For MGB owners

American MGC Register
34 Park Avenue
Ashville NC 28803
Phone: 704-274-2269
For MGC owners

North American MGB Register
PO Box MGB
Akin, IL
Phone: 800-NAMGBR-1
Fax: 618-438-2371
For MGB and Midget owners

North American MGA Register
2455 Glen Hill Drive
Indianapolis, IN 46420
For MGA owners, all models

ABOUT THE AUTHOR

Bill Harkins has been around MGs since college days in the early
'50's. His first MG, a 1950 TD was used while covering sports car
races, autoshows and classic cars as a free-lance writer and
photographer for <u>Motor Trend</u> magazine. He has raced, repaired
and restored a variety of MGs over the past 30 years. In addition
to being a member of several MG clubs in England and America,
he contributes to <u>The Sacred Octagon</u>, publication of the New
England "T" Register, the largest MG club in the US. He is
currently restoring two 1933 model J2 MGs at his home work-shop
in Fallbrook, California.

YEAR	LINE	Relative Condition: Worse ↔ Better		
		❸	❷	❶
1947—1949	TC Roadster	13500	16000	21000
1950—1953	TC Roadster	10000	13000	17000
1954—1955	TF Roadster	12000	15500	20500
1956—1959	A Roadster	6500	9000	14000
1957—1959	A Coupe	6000	8500	12000
1958—1960	A Twin-Cam Roadster	21000	28000	32000
1959—1961	A Twin-Cam Coupe	16000	24000	29000
1959—1961	A Mark I Roadster	6200	9400	13500
1961—1962	A Mark I Coupe	6000	8500	12000
1961—1962	A Mark II Roadster	7000	9500	13500
1961—1962	A Mark II Coupe	7000	9000	13000
1962	A Mark II Deluxe Coupe	13000	18500	24500
1962—1967	Midget Roadster	2500	3800	5250
1963—1969	B Roadster	3500	5000	8000
1967—1969	B GT Coupe	3000	4500	7800
1967—1969	C Roadster	6000	8700	11000
1967—1969	C GT Coupe	5000	8000	10000
1968—1974	Midget Roadster	2200	3300	4800
1970—1973	B Roadster	3000	4500	7500
1970—1973	B GT Coupe	3000	4500	7500

PORSCHE

BY COLE SCROGHAM

THE NAME AND THE CARS

"Porsche" as the name of a sports car conjures up several images in today's world. At the brink of a new century, Porsche personifies innovation and technological excellence. We tend to associate Porsche with ideas concerning design, engineering and a certain social status. In the beginning, however, Porsche was none of these things.

Ferdinand Porsche was born in an area of Austro-Hungary in 1875, nearly half a century before the First World War. It appears that the founder of Porsche was destined for some sort of design role from the start. He fitted his parents' house with electric wiring, and showed great interest in science and new ideas. Against his father's advice, Ferdinand traveled to Vienna near the turn of the century to study, and hopefully make something of himself. Porsche sold his services to others for many years, from Lohner to Daimler, Steyr, Volkswagen and others. The first design to bear his name, the Lohner-Porsche, featured an electric hub design and was completed when Porsche was only twenty-five years old. Truly this man was a brilliant engineer, but something was missing.

Ferdinand Porsche was certainly a brilliant designer, but he also possessed a searingly focused personality, one that wanted to be known for more than just designing cars. In the fall and winter of 1930, offices of a new company were opened in Stuttgart, Germany. This new company bore Porsche's name and was officially certified on March 6, 1931.

The first "Porsche" project was designated Type 7 (so that the Porsche engineers would not be seen as amateurs), completed for Wanderer. This project, and many others, would not bring Porsche notoriety in the early years, but would set the stage for a great new automotive design, the Volkswagen.

Porsche began work on the "Peoples' Car" concept in 1938, the same year that the Porsche team completed a move to Zuffenhausen, in the suburbs of Stuttgart. The success of the Volkswagen project would provide Porsche with much needed royalty payments and a higher profile in the automotive world. These elements would prove essential in the making of the Porsche sports car.

World War II gripped the Porsche contingent. The designers and engineers were actually split into three groups at one point to avoid any single calamity destroying the entire company. Many military projects, including the notorious Tiger tank, were spawned by the small company in those years, but Ferdinand Porsche was disappointed that the war had disrupted his company and his dream of a sports car bearing his name. Even more hardships were to arise, however, as Ferdinand was held by the allies following the war as a result of Pierre Peugeot's jealousy and other political maneuvering.

Porsche was eventually cleared, but his health was never the same, and he died in January of 1951. During the period of Ferdinand's illness, the fire behind Porsche was carried by his son, Ferdinand II, or Ferry. It was Ferry who masterminded the car project after the war in 1948, the project that brought his father's designs to life in the form of the Porsche 356. The first Porsche was a roadster with the curious placement of the engine in front of the gearbox. All of the subsequent 356 production cars would have the engine in the notorious rearward position.

Approximately 50 coupes preceded by the #1 roadster were hand-formed from aluminum in the town of Gmund, Austria. The men who made them had no concept of what they had created. After the Porsche roadster and Gmund coupes and the importation of the unique Porsche car into the United States through Max Hoffman, the fame of the Porsche began to grow. The lightweight body, alloy engine components and quick handling made the cars very enjoyable to drive. Of course, in the early 1950's there were indeed very few cars with those characteristics. The four cylinder engines were small but hardy, mated to a four-speed gearbox.

By today's standards, the 1950-1955 356's are unique and very interesting cars, but they only seem to stay that way if driven perhaps 30 minutes or so on a weekend. They are very slow, with 1300cc and 1500cc engines producing between 55 and 70 hp, and difficult to use in any circumstance other than touring. The pre-A (prior to 1956) cars do have an inherent value, however, if the car is complete and rust free. Most often these cars will be missing specific items, such as the unique integrated bumpers, or will have the incorrect engine and/or gearbox. These items can be purchased, but they are not Volkswagen parts, and in some cases are the most expensive Porsche parts to buy unless you have a limited production Porsche.

The other major point to consider is the spectre of rust. Almost any older car will have some sort of rust, but to Porsches this is critical because of the unibody construction. Seemingly simple rust repairs can be tremendously expensive (10% of the car's value and up), and NOS panels are extremely difficult to find. The good buy here is a reasonably original pre-A cabriolet with perhaps one repaint, making sure that rust is minimal and all of the parts are there. Also, keep in mind that there is probably a 356 of a different type with similar value that can be used and enjoyed to a greater extent. But the pre-A's value will tend to increase faster than most 356s because of their rarity.

One of Porsche's finest hours resulted in the creation of the Porsche speedster, built from 1954 until 1959. The speedster was designed after the 1952-1953 America roadsters. It was a very limited production run of all-aluminum roadsters that performed extremely well for the day. With this excellent design to build on and a total of fewer than 5000 speedsters made, the potential for a collectible piece is evident. The speedsters that are considered nice cars will always perform well, and if you catch a good price spike they can be very valuable to you as an investor. This will not become the object of your speedster ownership, however, for the speedster is a spectacular car to both own and drive on sunny days.

In any instance, the speedster is a spartan automobile, but wonderfully so. The speedster is what came to define Porsche in the 1950s, light, open and enjoyable. The 1954 and 1955 models are also classified as pre-As, and the same caveats apply here. There is a tremendous scarcity of parts for these cars, and they are in many respects unique. Be very careful of the "cheap" restoration project that is missing critical components. If there is any doubt as to what it takes to restore a pre-A speedster, visit a National Porsche Parade Concours and ask the poor soul who has one.

If you have your heart set on a pre-A coupe, cabriolet or speedster, try to locate one with a 1500cc engine. It will make your nearly impossible parts hunt slightly easier. Better yet, look for a more normal 1958 model speedster, the last year of non-Carrera speedster production, or a later coupe or cabriolet. With the introduction of the 356A model in 1956, things definitely made a turn for the better. The 1956 and 57 356As are the same car mechanically, still with the choice of coupe, cabriolet and speedster body options.

These cars, however, begin to drift away from the VW and toward a true Porsche sports car definition of their own. They are smooth road cars with refined transmissions and handling. The new 1600cc engine option dramatically improved torque and driveability, surprisingly with the best result in the normal, with 60hp. The normals do not have quite the zip of the super's 75hp, but they are very smooth and easy to drive. Nevertheless, the super is worth slightly more, if the correct engine in installed. These cars are capable of over 100mph, with the quick speedster taking just over 10 seconds to reach 60mph.

In 1957, the 356A body style was changed slightly to the T-2 body. The exhaust was routed through the bumper guards in the rear, and around this time the tail lights were changed to teardrop shape instead of four round "beehives". The 1958 and 1959 356As are the most collectible of this style, and are further refined to be an even nicer sports car. Basically, the caveats to buying a 356A include rust or collision damage. It is very difficult to conceal collision damage, and the rust is hard to combat. But parts are much easier to find for the 356As because of raw numbers, and they are a truly enjoyable car to drive.

The Porsche Carrera was introduced as a 356A model in 1956. The Carreras celebrated the success of Porsche racers at the Carrera Panamericana in Mexico. These 356-bodied cars were powered by the remarkable four-cam engine used in the 550 spyder, and are extremely rare and valuable cars. After 1957, the GT-optioned 356s featuring aluminum doors and deck lids and lightweight components become some of the most valuable production Porsches in existence. This does not include racing variants like the 550 spyder, RSK or Abarth Carrera.

Over the years, the Carrera was produced as 356A, B and C models. It becomes critical to consult noted professionals in restoration, as well as to contact the Porsche factory to authenticate and/or restore a Carrera. The four-cam engines are difficult to tune and very expensive to maintain. They're only a car for the serious collector, but virtually guaranteed to outperform the market in much the same manner as a limited production racer.

1959 Porsche 365A Carrera Speedster   *Leonard Turner Photo*

In 1960, the 356B was introduced in coupe and cabriolet versions. The last 32 GT speedsters were finished in 1959. The 356B models are identical in 1960 and 1961, and not as valuable as the 356A.

The 356Bs are, in some respects, the better equipped car with more features and a more modern design, but they lack the unique character of the As. A notable 356B design is the roadster, designed to replace the speedster, and the very limited production convertible D of 1959. Like the convertible D, the roadster had roll-up windows instead of the speedster's side curtains, but featured the 356B body style.

The 356B, with the new T-5 body, had a higher front fender line and more substantial bumpers for a more modern look. This design incorporated into the roadster made for a rather enjoyable top-down sports car. The chromed windshield frame is reminiscent of the speedster, but the revised shifter and more potent running gear is evident. The roadster has several unique parts to make the car special, so make sure you can locate them if they're not present on a car you are buying. Also look out for rust in your hunt for a nice original car.

Keep in mind that there are several hundred 1962 "twin-grille" roadsters out there that are even more valuable than the 1960-61 versions. Also introduced as an engine option in 1960 was the super-90 engine, producing 90hp and giving the 356's a bit more punch. The super-90 was a valuable option, and would carry the performance end of the 356 until the 356SC appeared in 1964.

In 1962, the 356B body was changed from the T-5 style to the T-6 style. This improvement allowed the gas tank to be filled from the outside for the first time, afforded more luggage space, featured two engine grilles instead of one and other detail items. The T-6 356Bs are approximately the same value as the T-5s, but allow many more conveniences if purchased to be a driver. More unique options, like sunroofs, are beginning to appear in these years. The T-6 cars are generally powered by the same powerplant as the 356As. 1600 normal and super engines had been the work horse for some years now with only minor modifications, but the super-90 was still offered as an engine option.

Be aware of the limited-edition Karmann-bodied coupes in both T-5 and T-6 bodies. These coupes look like a cabriolet with the hardtop in place, and are referred to as "notchbacks." For some maniacal reason, this relatively limited edition 356 is considerably less valuable than even a normal 356B coupe. Perhaps even Porsche owners have to draw the line at "weird." Following the 356B in 1964, the 356C would include many substantial innovations that make this model one of the most collectable and driveable early Porsches.

The 356C had the T-6 body, but featured disc brakes and two new engines. The 356C engine produced 75hp, while the 1600cc SC engine produced 95hp and was a quite potent car. The disc brakes were also a welcome change, and add a great deal to the package that a 356 has to offer. This explains the popularity of the 356C cabriolets. They are a highly refined 356 model that can be driven and will perform well even by modern standards. The 356C and SC models were the last of the 356s. In all, 76,300 of the inaugural Porsche type had been produced, including about 7,600 pre-As, 21,000 356As, 31,000 356Bs and a little fewer than 17,000 356Cs.

While the 356 was an admirable design, the time had come for a change. Porsche owners had been spoiled by the power of the Carrera 2 (a 2-1iter four-cam in a T-6 356 body), and also needed more room. The 901 was developed to satisfy these needs. The 901 produced 130hp as did the Carrera 2, and offered more room and comfort. The 901 was soon changed to the 911 after Peugeot complained about that sequence of numbers being planned for their new series, so the world would come to know this new Porsche as the 911. 911s were produced from 1964 with a 2-1iter 6-cylinder engine and a new five speed gearbox. They had disc brakes and adequate storage, and were altogether a fine design. Unstable handling quickly became their hallmark, however, as the extra engine weight prompted an exciting bit of oversteer near the limit.

The 1965-66 911s were also plagued with carburetor problems, usually solved by owners switching to Weber carburetors, as the Porsche factory did soon after. The Solexes would prove to be a sore point with many 911 owners, but the later Zenith and Weber versions were adequate. The early 911s were very prone to rust problems, especially in the front end, and since their value is not that great, you must exercise caution when searching for one of these cars. The 6-cylinder engine is also much more expensive to tune and repair than the four cylinder, so an early 911 is not a good choice for a daily driver in all seasons. They are, however, very unique cars, just as the 356As were, and are perhaps the best value out there for the money if you can find a really solid, original car. Buy good early 911s soon, while they are still relatively cheap.

1972 Porsche 911 Targa   *Leonard Turner Photo*

The 1967 911 was offered with a separate body option other than the coupe; the "Targa" celebrated Porsche's dominance of the Targa Florio road race in Sicily. In 1967 only, the Targa was also offered with a soft rear window, but typically the large rear glass and roll bar point out the Targa. Naturally, as with any convertible, the Targa is prone to leak around the top to door glass sealing area. This leak, and a moisture attracting area just behind the upper doors on the quarter panels, make for added rust problems that should be checked thoroughly in any potential acquisition. 1967 was also the first year of the 911S (Super), which at 160hp was quite an impressive performer and is highly sought after.

Look out for 1968, when emissions required a smog pump and other atrocities that detract from the performance of the 2-1iter engine. The 911S also disappears for one year only, replaced in 1968 by the 911L (Luxury). The 911T (Touring) would make an appearance to take over for the 911, and the 911E (Einspritzung or injected) would be the middle range for the 911 in 1969. Any unusual variation, like a 1967 soft-rear-window 911S, is particularly valuable in-these years of alphabet soup.

As if Porsche anticipated reliability and cost problems with the 911, the 912 with basically a 1600SC engine was also offered from 1965-'69. The maintenance was much more convenient, and all of the rest of the 912 was identical to the 911, making this car a good bargain for a driver. The 912s are now close to the 911 in value, and should be, for they are more usable and have that old 356 spirit. The early 1965 912s even have a three-gauge painted dash as the 356 did, before the 911 design was adopted with the five-gauge wood dash. Look for a good 1967 or 1969 912.

1976 Porsche 912E   *Leonard Turner Photo*

The 911 became another car in 1969, as the wheelbase was lengthened to help cure the handling problem. The solution worked, and 1969 and later cars are much easier to drive quickly.

The 1969 912s are also equipped with this body. For 1970, the 912 was discontinued and the 911 became a 2.2-liter. The 911s, particularly the 911S, became more and more powerful, culminating in the 190hp, 2.4-liter of 1973. The S and E models even sported some aluminum components in the rear to save weight, as did the 356 GTs. The 1972 models were all equipped with the new 2.4-liter engine for the T, E and S, but a peculiar movement of the oil tank access into the rear quarter panel makes these cars less desirable.

On the good side, a new transmission, the 915, allowed the first four gears to be in the classic H pattern and improved shifting action. This almost makes up for the leaking oil tank, but the 1973 models had it all figured out, and these are the most desirable, with the oil tank access back in its rightful position inside the fender. Typically, the S is a difficult car to drive, as the engine must be operated at high revs before it is becomes efficient and stops lunging. The T is the most docile, but lacks brute horsepower. Perhaps the best choice is the injected E. It is powerful and tractable in nearly every situation. The E is equipped with an injection pump (as are 1973 911Ts) that can be troublesome and expensive to rebuild. They are generally rebuilt along with the engine, a point to check on a "mechanically perfect" 911E. The 1973 911T injection signaled the onset of CIS fuel injection, which would continue until the Motronic 911's in 1984. The CIS system is a good system, but beware of pumping the gas pedal during starting and ruining the air box, a costly fix.

The 912 faded to make room for a new entry level Porsche, the 914. This joint Porsche-VW project would be a financial disaster for VW and a disaster of prestige for Porsche. The 1970 to 1972 four-cylinder 914's were overpriced, slow and very difficult to shift correctly. The saving grace in those years was the 914-6, powered by the 911T engine, and making about 110hp. The six was still overpriced and difficult to shift, but the engine note and exceptional handling makes this 914 a collectible car. A limited production run of 914-6 GTs was made for club racing purposes, identified by the 916-style steel flared fenders and flush bumpers. As you might expect, these GTs are very collectible and very rare, but certainly are the ultimate 914.

Almost every 914 was prone to a leaking battery and subsequent rust in the lower structure. This is a major point to be aware of. In any instance, the four-cylinder 914s prior to 1973 are to be avoided. The 1973 914s were led by the capable 2-liter four-cylinder model, but also produced in a 1.7 and 1.8-liter version. The shift linkages were redesigned, and the 90hp 2.0 was a fine little sports car through 1974. The 1975 and 1976 cars lack the character of the 1973s, and are burdened with emissions equipment and less powerful engines, as well as huge crash bumpers that take away from the clean design.

1973 Porsche 914   *Leonard Turner Photo*

Generally, the 1973 2.0 is the car to collect and drive anywhere. It is a delightful little car, but 911 owners will never let you associate with them. On the bright side, a mid-engined two-seater with a convertible top, strong engine and four-wheel disc brakes is quite a lot of car for the money. Just do not expect to consider yourself a collector by owning one unless it is a low-mileage or spectacular example.

After 1973, things went downhill for Porsche and the rest of the automotive world. The Arab oil shock and emissions requirements wrought havoc with the sports car industry, and Porsche was no exception. Also, crash testing mandated the use of energy absorbing bumpers, most obvious on the 911 line, as they disrupted the classic look of the car and replaced it with a modern one. The new 1974 engines were all 2.7-liter engines, and, burdened as they were for fuel economy, they were one of the worst 6-cylinder engine designs offered by Porsche. The 911 and 911S were offered in 1974, the 911S from 1975 to 1977. These cars are prone to overheating, poor performance, and questionable reliability.

The only positive note in this time period is the resurrection of the Carrera and the elimination of most of the rust problem by zinc treatment of bodies in 1976. The Carrera RS was offered as a limited production racer in 1973 in lightweight and touring trim, and today they are quite valuable. The 1974 Carrera, with its characteristic ducktail rear spoiler, was not a racer, but with 210hp the Carrera was far superior to the other 2.7 engined 911s. The 1975 Carrera was probably the most aggressive looking 911 to date with wider flares, a full whale tail and front spoiler. Other than being excessively heavy, this Carrera signaled a bright spot for the future of Porsche in both performance and styling. The 1975 Carrera would help announce the radical Turbo Carrera for 1976, a Porsche that is valuable but nearly as difficult as a four-cam to rely on and pay for maintenance.

Generally, the 1974-1977 911S can be treated as the 914s are. They have a great deal of redeeming characteristics, including CIS fuel injection and impeccable road manners, but the car as a whole is just not a collectible piece in the current day unless you have a very nice example. Granted, it is hard to find a 911 that is usable as a daily commuter for a reasonable sum, but this 911 series should always be regarded as the Porsche 911s weakest years.

After 1977, Porsche was back on target, and the 1978 and 1979 911SCs are some of the most usable Porsches ever built. The 3.0 engine is marvelous, and while these cars are not yet collectibles, they are very fine road cars to keep an eye on. Porsche continually builds cars that will be collectible, because Porsche is quite good at selling small unique runs of cars. Take, for example, the 1980 Weissach 911SC, the 1983 911 cabriolet, the 1989 speedster and the 1992 American roadster. Porsche is a unique company with a commitment to building high quality automobiles in small numbers. All this adds up to some very collectible Porsches in the future as well as now.

After the 914 series expired in 1976, Porsche needed a model to take over the low price line under the 911. For one year in 1976, the 912 took over this slot. The 912E was essentially a 1976 911 body powered by a 2.0 914 engine, and these are not well-known because of their short life span. These cars have held their value well but lack promise because of a basic incompatibility with Porsche's overall goal to build high-performance and advanced cars. The 912E was an antique design even by 1976 standards, and although the cars have much to offer, including all the 911 refinements to be found elsewhere, they do not stand to become above-average investment.

With the demise of the 912E, Porsche combined with Audi to introduce the much-heralded 924, a totally new concept for Porsche. But, this project was destined to come apart, much as the joint Porsche-VW 914 project did. The 924 was radical by Porsche's standard; the engine was in the front, and it was water-cooled, basically an Audi-designed engine in a Porsche car.

While the 924 body took some impressive steps in aerodynamics and weight balance, there was always something lacking with the car. Mostly there was a dearth of horsepower, and the 924 quickly became relegated to duty as gifts for college graduates, and the model was rejected by the Porsche purist.

Even the 924 turbo, which made up significant ground in power output, was a busy car that had a bad habit of destroying turbochargers at frequent intervals. Altogether, the 924 was a car that Porsche wanted to forget, and the collector should forget it as well, with the exception of one car. The 1977 924 Sebring could well be a good investment if you can find an excellent example with no rust and low miles. The Sebring special edition was finished in white with Martini red and blue striping. The interiors were a rather loud red, trimmed in Martini blue. These special edition cars celebrated the Sebring, Florida 12-hour victories that Porsche posted (under Martini-Rossi sponsorship, of course).

While the 924 was a disaster in the minds of Porschephiles, it paved the way for a more accepting attitude toward the 924's successor, the 944. This car was introduced in 1983, during an era when Porsche produced more cars than it ever had before, or likely ever will again. Thus, raw numbers play against the 944 as a collector car, but were in Porsche's favor during the first few years of production. The 944 was introduced at a price of $18,750, and they could not keep inventory in the showrooms. The 944 was what the 924 should have been, with a torque 2.5-liter, four-cylinder engine, an aggressive body shape and impressive handling. The possibility that the 944 will become a collector's car remains in doubt, however.

1983 Porsche 944 Coupe   *Leonard Turner Photo*

The 944 design was helped in late 1985 with a new dash layout and the powerful turbo and turbo S models. These were impressive, but they suffer the same fate as all the Porsche water-cooled cars; they depreciate rapidly, except for the nice cabriolet version. Whether this trend will reverse is open to speculation, as these cars are bought as daily transportation and used without consideration for their possible collectibility. If you want to buy one to collect, look for original paint and low mileage, preferably a post-1985 944S (16-valve engine) or turbo. Be wary of poorly-maintained cars in any case, as 944s require periodic drive-belt tensioning, and tend to have problems with water pumps, tensioners and power-steering lines.

As the 944 occupied the lower price slot for Porsche, another new design took over a position above the bread-and-butter 911 in 1978. The 928 was hailed as a true water-cooled Porsche, and even garnered Car-Of-The-Year honors from the motoring press when introduced. The 928 had moved through several stages of evolution, but has always maintained a distinguished character that combines a powerful engine with relative luxury for a Porsche. The interior is spacious for two occupants, and the car is very well thought out for the touring set.

Although the five-speed version offers the best performance, a high percentage of 928s were ordered with the optional four-speed automatic that takes full advantage of the big eight's torque response. While the 928 has proven to be tough and relatively problem-free, if any expense is incurred, it will be large. The parts cost for 928s is prohibitive, and their saving grace is that they rarely have problems if properly maintained.

The culmination of the 928 came with the S4 in the late 1980s. The 928 S4 and the lighter GT variant have a 32-valve four-cam engine, stiffer suspension and redesigned nose and tail sections. Everyone agrees that the S4 is one of the finest touring designs that Porsche has created; the only negative is the cost. Look for a nice 928 S4 you can afford that's a few years old, and drive it sparingly. It should become more valuable, simply because Porsche is producing them in small numbers.

1985 Porsche 928S   *Leonard Turner Photo*

There's no cabriolet version of the 928, perhaps a mistake on Porsche's part, but nonetheless a reality. Note that the 1985 and later 928Ss were equipped with the tamer 32-valve engine and ABS brakes (offered as options on Euro 1984 models). Beware of a car that has a history of tensioner or unusual electrical problems. And, should you wish a 928, be sure to play the depreciation game to your advantage, remembering that water-cooled Porsche's tend to depreciate more rapidly than their air-cooled brothers. And, be patient, because the Porsche you buy will become more than just a car to you.

How To Join The Club

Any serious interest in Porsches should begin with a membership in Porsche Club of America, 5530 Edgemont Drive, Alexandria, VA 22310.

WHERE TO GO FOR PARTS

G&W Motorwerkes, Ltd.
Special Interest Parts/356 and Carrera, early 911
Concours/Vintage Racing/Sales of unique Porsches
703-942-5285/Fax: 703-942-4040

Porsche Vintage
Parts for 356, 914, early 911 of adequate quality
800-252-4444 for nearest dealer

Stoddard Porsche
Highly involved Porsche Vintage dealer
Specialize in 356, 911
800-342-1414/Fax: 216-946-9410

Brumos Porsche   Later model Porsche items
800-726-9155/Fax: 904-725-5006

Imparts
Numerous parts for all types
800-325-904/Fax: 314-962-3250

Autothority
Later model performance parts
703-323-0919

Zim's
Parts for all models at competitive prices
800-356-2964

PMO
911 Weber dealer
213-393-5423

Parts Obsolete
Special interest/356 parts
714-540-2383

Vasek Polak
Special interest parts/All models
213-376-7434

Tweeks
356, early 911, other Porsche parts
800-428-2200

Andial
All models/Performance applications
714-957-3900

International Mercantile
Quality rubber/All models
619-438-2205

ABOUT THE AUTHOR

Cole Scrogham's interest in Porsches began early in the family restoration and race prep business. After graduating university with honors, he devoted full time to the business, and has completed restorations of 356 GSs and GTs, 550 spyder, 904, 911, 914, 911 speedster, etc. Cole's first love is the 356 and he's doing a book on the 356 Carrera. He also races occasionally, writes for <u>Porsche Panorama</u>, <u>Excellence</u> and the <u>356 Registry</u>, and enjoys judging concours at national club events.

YEAR	LINE	Relative Condition: Worse ↔ Better		
		❸	❷	❶
1950—1955	356 Coupe	12000	16000	20000
1950—1955	356 Cabriolet	27000	35500	41000
1955	356 Speedster	36000	44000	52000
1950—1955	356 Super Coupe	13000	17500	21000
1950-1955	356 Super Cabriolet	32000	38000	44000
1955	365 Super Speedster	40000	51000	60000
1956—1959	356A Coupe	9500	14500	18500
1956—1959	356A Cabriolet	23000	31000	36500
1956—1959	356A Speedster	35000	40000	49000
1956—1959	356A Super Coupe	11000	15500	19500
1956—1959	356A Super Cabriolet	29000	34000	41000
1956—1959	356A Super Speedster	41000	50000	62000
1960—1962	356B Coupe	9500	13500	18500
1960—1962	356B Cabriolet	24000	28000	35000
1960—1962	356B Roadster	34000	42000	47000
1960—1962	356B Super Coupe	11500	15500	20000
1960—1962	356B Super Cabriolet	29000	34000	42000
1960—1962	356B Super Roadster	36500	46000	53500
1963—1965	356C Coupe	10000	14500	19000
1963—1965	356C Cabriolet	25000	30000	37000
1963—1965	356C Super Coupe	12000	16500	21000
1963—1965	356C Super Cabriolet	28000	34000	44000

YEAR	LINE	Relative Condition: Worse ↔ Better		
		❸	❷	❶
1965—1969	912 Coupe	6500	9000	12500
1965—1969	912 Targa	7500	9000	13000
1965—1967	911 Coupe	8000	10500	15000
1965—1967	911 Targa	8000	11000	16000
1967	911S Coupe	11000	14000	20000
1967	911S Targa	10500	15000	20000
1970—1975	9141.7-8 Targa	2800	4500	6500
1970—1971	914/6 Targa	9000	13500	17000
1973—1975	914 2.0 Targa	3700	5000	7500
1968 —1973	911 Coupe	7000	9500	14000
1968—1973	911 Targa	7500	9500	14500
1968—1973	911T Coupe	7000	9500	14000
1968—1973	911T Targa	7500	9500	14500
1969—1973	911E Coupe	7500	10500	15000
1969—1973	911E Targa	8000	11000	15500
1969—1973	911S Coupe	10500	16000	19000
1969—1973	911S Targa	11000	15500	20000
1974—1977	911 Coupe	8000	12000	15500
1974—1977	911 Targa	8500	12500	16500
1974—1977	911S Coupe	9000	12500	16500
1974—1977	911S Targa	9500	13000	17000
1974—1975	Carrera Coupe	12000	16500	20000
1974—1975	Carrera Targa	13000	17000	22000

TRIUMPH

BY MIKE COOK

PRACTICAL DRIVING FUN

There are really two histories of Triumph cars. One is the story of a German immigrant who arrived in England before the turn of the century and founded a bicycle business that prospered and became a car company. The other is a post-World-War-Two tale featuring a hard-headed industrial magnate with a preference for simple styling and low cost, and a series of potent little two-seater sports cars.

Siegfried Bettman began manufacturing Triumph bicycles in Coventry in 1897, first for export and then for a growing domestic market. Under the influence of his partner, engineer Mauritz Schulte, the beginning of the well-remembered Triumph motorcycle came in 1902, when a small motor was first added to a Triumph bicycle with a reinforced frame. Triumph bikes were a successful enterprise, but Triumph management was also looking at cars and produced their first four-wheeler in 1923. At the time, their two-wheeled products were famous in England and Europe and the firm was building as many as 15,000 units a year for military and civilian use.

Bettman, in 1919, had brought in Claude V. Holbrook, an officer with whom he had dealt in selling motorcycles to the military during World War Two, to manage Triumph. The automobile business was developed under Holbrook's direction, although Bettman was with the firm until 1933.

Triumph's first car was the 10/20 and it was praised by the press and owners for its excellent workmanship and finish. It was not made to be a hot performer but was intended for reliability. The numerical designation was made up of the taxable horsepower and the actual bhp.

Sold under the slogan "The Quality Light Car," 1920s Triumphs were tall and square but featured fine materials, more equipment than their competitors and occasional innovations such as the first British use of four-wheel hydraulic brakes, on the 13/35 Tourer of 1925. However, the company achieved more fame when it introduced a sporty little open car in 1927, the Triumph Super Seven.

Triumph's Super Seven competed with the Austin and Morris popular light cars in the late 1920s and early 1930s. Offered in several factory open and sedan versions, the Super Seven was well received in the press and was a regular subject for custom bodywork. Powered by a tiny 832cc four-cylinder engine, the car had a four-speed gearbox, four-wheel hydraulic brakes and full instrumentation, a high level of equipment for such a low-priced car. The Super Seven was produced until 1934.

Owners raced special-bodied Sevens against the MG and Austin 750cc class cars, but Triumph really shone in rallying. Donald Healey, just beginning his career in the motor industry, finished seventh overall with a Super Seven in the Monte Carlo Rally in 1929 and won several British events in the next two years, all this with a car which would not reach 50 mph!

The Super Seven's ruggedness and reliability were well demonstrated by various owners in drives across the United States, Canada and Australia, often non-stop over terrible roads. Despite this performance, sales were slow and production remained low. Austin and Morris Sevens were built by the thousands while Triumph seldom topped 150 per week.

Joining an industry trend towards very small displacement six-cylinder engines (the "light six"), Triumph introduced the Scorpion sedan for 1931. Lasting only two years, this model scored well on styling and features but, being basically a Seven with a larger, heavier engine, the handling was poor. It was the last of the early, conservative Triumphs.

In 1933 Siegfried Bettman was asked by the Triumph Board to retire in order to allow Col. Holbrook to attempt to revive sales with a new product philosophy. Triumphs, from that time on would be designed and built as performers and marketed to appeal to the sporting driver. Donald Healey was hired as Technical Director. He would influence the sporting character of the cars through the remainder of the 1930s, winning quite a few trophies in the process.

Triumph's Super Nine was the first to carry out the sporting philosophy. Powered by a Coventry Climax designed engine, this series offered Triumph's first factory sports car. Triumph's most successful export market was Australia and the new sportster was dubbed the Southern Cross. With an aluminum body, near 70 mph capability and Triumph's long list of standard equipment, this car looked like a winner.

The Ten HP chassis of the Southern Cross was used for a range of sedans as well but this was soon replaced by an all-new range named "Gloria". Introduced in 1933, the Gloria name carried Triumph to its pre-war peak of performance and styling. With Donald Healey at the wheel, a Gloria scored third overall in the Monte Carlo Rally and the model won its class in the Monte and other events many times.

Gloria styling was by Walter Belgrove, who had joined the company in 1927, and would be the only Triumph manager to continue his association with the marque after World War II. Models in the Gloria range from 1935 through 1937 included four and six-cylinder sports two-seaters and tourers, four-door sedans, drop heads and a selection of custom-bodied sedans made by various coachbuilders.

Other ranges offered by Triumph in the late 1930s were the Vitesse line of sedans and, finally, the high-performance Dolomites, named after an experimental straight-eight supercharged sports car created by Donald Healey in 1934. Never produced due to lack of funds for development, the eight was Healey's mount in a number of European rallies.

Featuring an American-style cast "waterfall" grille, similar to the Hudson Terraplane, the Dolomites were all-steel, sleekly-styled luxury cars in the same class as the smaller Jaguars. They featured new, overhead valve four and six-cylinder engines designed and built by Triumph. Once again, the press gave them high praise but there were few buyers and production hardly reached 2000 in the best years. Both the bicycle and motorcycle portions of the business had been sold to raise cash as Triumph went deeper into debt.

Triumph offered as many as seventeen different models in 1937 and 1938. Just about any combination of engine and body that a customer wanted was available - anything to sell a car! However, as war broke out in Europe in 1939, the Triumph Motor Company went into receivership and the assets were sold. The two main production facilities were destroyed in air raids along with all the spare parts stock and most of the records. After the War, the assets and the name were purchased by the Standard Motor Company Ltd. and the second part of the history of Triumph cars began with the creation of the Standard-Triumph Motor Company Ltd.

Many pre-war Triumphs are of interest to collectors but very few exist and virtually none are in the United States. The later open sports models, such as the Southern Cross, were built in very small numbers and few of any model survived the scrap drives during World War Two. Keeping an eye on British collectors publications and contacting the various Triumph clubs and registers would be the best way to spot pre-war Triumphs for sale. Prices for the later sedans in top condition will range from $15,000 to $30,000. Roadsters will be a matter of negotiation due to their rarity. Spare parts are unobtainable as are drawings and technical material, most of which disappeared in the wartime destruction. However, despite the difficulties, the brilliant styling alone would make ownership of one of these rare cars quite rewarding.

Collecting Triumphs of the 1945-on era is quite a different matter and the enthusiast will find a variety of styles and categories from which to choose, many of which have good availability of spare parts. Further, there are active Triumph clubs covering virtually every series and still enjoying the camaraderie so desirable to the sports car enthusiast.

Triumph sedans played a smaller part in the development of the popularity of the marque in the post war years. While the Triumph Motor Company had been mainly home market oriented, Standard-Triumph was an export-hungry manufacturer looking for volume sales and they found that volume in the United States. What created the demand? The post-war sports car craze and the Triumph TR series.

The second history of Triumph cars began with the decision by Sir John Black, managing director and deputy chairman of the Standard Motor Company, to acquire the remains of the Triumph Motor Company. The formation of Standard-Triumph with Black as both chairman and managing director was Black's way to get into the building of sports and luxury cars. Having watched with envy the progress of Jaguar, Black could now proceed with his own highly styled performance cars. The Triumph 1800 roadster and saloon were announced in the fall of 1946.

Both cars were powered with the 1776cc four-cylinder overhead valve engine built by Standard for Jaguar. Both were built on a chassis using tubular members on which was mounted the suspension from the Standard Flying Twelve. However, the bodies bore no resemblance to Standards, and could wear the Triumph badge secure in the knowledge that no other car on British roads looked the least bit similar.

Styling for the roadster was done at Standard Triumph by Frank Callaby. It was his first styling job and came close to exaggerating the classic sports car lines popularized in the 1930s. The radiator sat well back between the front fenders. The headlights were large units mounted separately on either side of the radiator grille. There were no running boards but the flowing fender lines were still suggestive of them. Certainly, the body construction, aluminum and steel panels over ash wood frames, was traditional but the car had its own unique features.

Triumph 1800 Roadster   *Triumph Photo*

There was a single bench seat which would hold three people. A column gear shift was standard. Finally, the new 1800 had to be the last car ever built with a "dickey seat". Known as a rumble seat in the USA, this installation had been popular in the 1930s and Triumph's last sportster, the Dolomite roadster/coupe, had featured one in 1937. In the 1800 there were two small seats which were exposed by opening the trunk lid. The forward section of the rear deck also lifted up and was provided with windows so that the rear occupants had their own windshield.

Walter Belgrove, Triumph's stylist, had joined Standard but was not involved with the design of the 1800 roadster. His part in the rebirth of Triumph was to style the 1800 sedan to Sir John Black's taste with formal "razor-edge" lines like limousines of the period. What he came up with was a severe but attractive slab-sided car which remained in production until 1954, five years after the last roadster was built. Later known as the Renown, the new sedan lacked only size to make it match the formal limousines of the day in elegance.

The two Triumphs were among the last few coach-built production models built in the world and they made their mark. Handicapped by low performance, even after a 2088cc engine was installed in 1949, they nonetheless perpetuated the Triumph name until the new company had a chance to make a more modern car. Considering the unusual styling and limited production they are currently fairly inexpensive. The saloons are particularly reasonable, selling for under $10,000, while the roadsters have been known to sell for more than $25,000. Parts can be found but items like the huge steel front fenders are simply not available.

At the start of the 1950s, the new Triumph company was drawing close to production of the first TR sports car. However, there was one more interesting step to be taken and in concept it was one that few companies would have risked. The next Triumph was an economy sedan the size of a VW Beetle but with the razor-edge styling of the Renown. The Triumph Mayflower was possibly the most unusual small car to be produced since 1945.

Intended for export as well as home consumption, the Mayflower was in many ways a desirable package. The classic upright styling was hard to execute on an 84.5-inch wheelbase, but was managed through cooperative efforts between Mulliners, who built the Renown bodies and Walter Belgrove. It featured pressed-steel, unit-body construction and was as solid a vehicle as any on the market. The car would hold four in comfort despite its small size and had good luggage room. An American style three-speed column shift helped the interior room but did not assist the old-fashioned, flat-head, 1247cc engine. Although the Mayflower did well around town, highway performance was dismal and it could not keep up with American traffic.

Mayflowers were popular in England but sales did not hold up and the car went out of production in 1953. Nearly 35,000 were built, and enough survive to support an active Mayflower Club. Although nearly 5,000 reached Canada and the United States, hard driving and road salt finished most of them. The sturdy unit body was not rust-proofed, and once rot has set in there is no way to repair the structure without building a body jig. Since the engine was unique to the car, parts are hard to come by. The gearbox and rear axle components were shared with other company products.

The biggest appeal of the Mayflower is that it is **cute**. No other small car had the custom-body look of this miniature limousine with its classic radiator grille, large glass area and roomy interior. They are reasonably priced in the collecting market as well, selling from about $2500 to perhaps $5000. The Mayflower could be that "different" car you have been looking for.

As the Triumph Mayflower approached the end of production, Triumph's first post-war sports car was in the concept stage and its debut was planned for the 1953 Earls Court Motor Show in London. It was born of the need for Standard-Triumph to increase profitable exports, which the Mayflower had not accomplished, and of Sir John Black's passion to match or beat the success of MG, Jaguar, and even Morgan, in producing successful sports models. Typically, he attempted to get the project going with very low investment in tooling and maximum use of parts and technology on hand.

The original show car was built on a modified 1939 Standard Flying Nine chassis, adapted to take Mayflower front suspension and rear axle and the four-speed version of the Standard Vanguard gearbox. Power came from a 1991cc version of the Vanguard four-cylinder, wet-liner engine. It had an 88-inch wheelbase. The body, quickly designed by Belgrove, had a simple opening at the front for cooling, slab sides, cut-down doors and a bob-tail with no trunk and the spare wheel recessed into the back panel. The front accurately predicted the eventual production car. The rear, fortunately, did not survive past the prototype.

This "quick and dirty" creation did not get raves at Earls Court but it did create interest. The talk of 100 mph performance and low price put a gleam in enough eyes to make Black re-think his original ideas of limited production and treat the car as a volume production job. Re-styling was begun and ex-BRM tester Ken Richardson was hired to do the road testing and development work. After months of effort, the first production prototypes emerged in time for the Geneva Show in March. Richardson drove one, specially prepared, at 124 mph on the Jabbeke highway in

Belgium to prove the performance claims. Real production got underway in July and, from the beginning, the majority of the cars were left hand drive, destined for the United States.

Originally code-named the "20TS Project", the new car was a "TR2" by the time it went on sale. The prototype was retroactively called "TR1" but never actually had that designation. These TRs, as they were soon called by enthusiasts everywhere, came into almost instant popularity. In a few short years, the term TR was so identified with sports cars that the TRW corporation ran ads noting that TRW was NOT a small British sports car!

1953 was a year of transition for the sports car market in the United States. America's interest in two seaters that were fun to drive was frustrated by the attractive but old-fashioned and slow MG TD, and piqued by the Jaguar XK-120 which, at over $3000, was well out of reach of most enthusiasts. A demand existed for an affordable, quick and attractive two-seater.

Several car makers were poised to fill this gap and Triumph managed to get there first. The styling could be criticized but the overall appearance was neat and eye-catching. The TR2 was certainly quick, handled reasonably well, gave excellent fuel mileage and even had luggage space. The top, still rudimentary, nevertheless kept out the rain when properly erected, the car was rugged and the price, under $2500, was right.

At the same time as the TR1 was being shown, Donald Healey, now running his own car company, had exhibited a new sports car design which was snapped up by the British Motor Corporation and named the Austin Healey 100. This was in production and there were Sunbeam sports cars on the horizon as well. Triumph was going to have to work to keep up with the competition and did so in two primary ways.

First, the company entered the TR2s in major European rallies and at Le Mans. Overall wins usually eluded them, but class victories were common, and it was a great way to demonstrate the car's ruggedness. These factory-prepared cars were supervised and frequently driven by Ken Richardson and were good illustrations of the "win on Sunday, sell on Monday" philosophy. They also provided testing for technical innovations, one of which put Triumph way ahead of its rivals. Competition successes in European rallies and racing, particularly in the United States, were always part of the company's marketing strategy for the TR series.

Triumph TR3   *Triumph Photo*

Technical advances were the second means Triumph had of keeping ahead of the competition. Initially, the TR2 was merely tidied up as it went along. The original doors, which went all the way to the bottom of the body and would hit the curb, trapping the driver in the car, were shortened during 1955. In 1956, a TR3 was announced with a cross-barred grille, more horsepower and an optional rear seat. It was the 1957 model that leaped ahead, however, with the introduction of front disc brakes for the first time on a British production car. Developed at Le Mans, these brakes were a tremendous selling point and really boosted sales. Other touches, like sliding plexiglass windows in the side curtains made the car more comfortable.

For 1958, the car became a TR3A and had a new front panel with a wide grille and sturdier bumper. This continued through 1961. 1962, final year for the TR3, brought the TR3B. Produced only for the United States as a means of using up the last of the TR3 bodies, most of the Bs had the optional "2.2" (2167cc) engine and the new all-synchro gearbox developed for the TR4.

The TR2 had been an ingenious combination of available components assembled on a new chassis with some new engineering and clothed in a simple body. Nine years later, the TR4 came about in virtually the identical way, yet managed to appear a totally new car.

Based on the TR3 chassis, the TR4 had a 4" wider track which allowed better passenger space and gave better handling. It used the 2167cc engine. The body, which featured roll-up windows and was styled by Michelotti of Italy, was the end result of several design exercises involving longer, more luxurious cars. In the end, Standard Triumph management went for simplicity and low cost.

Sales were poor at the beginning of the 1960s and the company was losing money. In April, 1961, Standard-Triumph was taken over by the Leyland Motor Corporation, a large truck and bus manufacturer. Alick Dick, who had replaced Sir John Black as Managing Director, left the company that year. Just at that point, Triumph scored another publicity success at Le Mans, winning the team prize in 1961. The cars used, specially-built fiberglass units called the "TRS", were equipped with a special twin-cam experimental engine and looked remarkably like the TR4.

The TR4, introduced as a 1962 model, restored energy to Triumph export sales. It offered the amenities which American motorists seemed to prefer and equalled the features of the MG, its chief competitor, while out-performing it. The TR4 continued in production, unchanged except for details of seats, carburetors, etc., through 1964.

The one feature of the TR4 that still limited buyer enthusiasm was the ride. Harsh as the TR3, it was impossible to improve while still using the solid rear axle mounted above the frame rails. Triumph engineers produced a solution in the form of a trailing-arm independent rear suspension adapted from the Triumph 2000 sedan. Using a new chassis frame with the same 88-inch wheelbase, the TR4A models appeared in 1965 and the additional comfort was noticeable. Interestingly, the US distributors felt that the $150 higher price would hurt sales and asked for a straight-axle version of the TR4A as well. This was produced with the same small styling changes and no IRS badge on the trunk for the same price as the 1964 TR4.

Power was the next problem. Other manufacturers were producing smoother engines than Triumph's four and with buyer sophistication growing, some technical advances were needed. The company was building a six-cylinder engine for its large sedans which, in 2.5-liter form, offered excellent power and torque and would fit into the TR with minimal alterations.

Triumph TR 250   *Triumph Photo*

Installation of the six-cylinder engine produced the TR5 and TR250 which were in production for one model year, 1968. The TR5, with fuel-injection, was a UK-Europe model only. With 140 brake horsepower, it was a stormer but the fuel injection would have added several hundred dollars to the retail price of the car, hard to justify in the competitive North American market. Thus, the TR250, with distinctive exterior trim and badging, came to the United States in twin-carburetor form. Horsepower was only 106, but more torque made the car much more pleasant to drive and the smooth roar of the exhaust was a delight to enthusiasts.

A further re-do of the TR was presented to the world for 1969. Styled by Karmann in Germany, the new TR6 was a transformation and a thoroughly modern car. Underneath, the frame was TR4A. The doors and windshield were the same as the 1962 TR4, but the smart, squared-off lines made it a car for the 1970s. The removable steel hardtop would turn the car into a snug coupe. Even air conditioning, installed at US ports of entry, was optional although there was still no automatic transmission. TR6s were produced with carburetors for the US and fuel injection for the rest of the world, through 1976.

Starting in 1975, Triumph launched the TR7 as a replacement for the TR6. The original TR series cars remain much more interesting to the collector, however, and should be reviewed as a group. They were produced in large enough quantities to make them readily available, and most parts can be obtained, including virtually all body panels, rubber parts, etc. Many enthusiast clubs exist like the Vintage Triumph Register in the United States.

Restoration of any TR2 through TR6 can be accomplished by the hobbyist due to the simplicity of the car. Almost everything is "bolt-on". When looking for a suitable project car, watch for rust in the area behind the front wheels where water can intrude between inner and outer fenders. Floors can rot out and the upper portions of the rear fenders can rust. The panel forward of the fuel filler on TR4-TR6 models is rust-susceptible also. However, even if much of the body needs replacement, the separate chassis frame still makes restoration possible. Best of all, cars of all models in the series, in good condition, can be obtained for under $10,000. Prices overseas, due to limited supply, are much higher. Restored TRs are strong, fun to drive and keep up very well with modern traffic.

Triumph TR6   *Triumph Photo*

A number of custom cars were built on TR chassis, the most interesting of which was the Triumph Italia. A very pretty coupe styled by Michelotti, the Italia was put into production by Vignale using TR3 chassis and running gear supplied directly by Standard-Triumph. About 300 were built in 1959 and 60 and they demand good prices today due to their Ferrari-like styling and despite the impossibility of obtaining body parts.

The Standard Motor Company had always based its sales success on small family cars and this philosophy had been applied once to Triumph via the Mayflower. In the 1950s, Standard produced the Eight and Ten sedan and station wagon. Very stark and utilitarian, these vehicles wore Triumph badges in the United States in the 1958-62 period. However, the company had set a goal to produce a modern small car and when it appeared in 1959, it bore the Triumph name.

Actually the first Triumph to be styled by Giovanni Michelotti, the Herald had a backbone chassis with bolt-on body, 948cc overhead-valve engine, four-speed all-synchro gearbox and all-independent suspension with swing axles at the rear. Launched as a two-door sedan and coupe, the line shortly included a four-passenger convertible. It was a forward-looking design which became quite popular and stayed in production until 1971. Several thousand, mainly convertibles, were sold in the United States.

Not a collector's car, the Herald spawned two variations which certainly are; the Triumph Spitfire and the GT6. Spitfires came on the market in 1963, competing directly with the MG Midget and Austin-Healey Sprite, and were built continuously through 1980. Again from Michelotti, the cute little Spitfire had a twin-carb 1147cc version of the Herald engine, four-speed gearbox, the independent suspension, roll-up windows and virtually the same passenger and luggage room as its big brother, the TR4! It used the TR4 windscreen. Like the Herald, it had a one-piece hood/front fender unit which lifted forward to expose engine and front suspension.

Triumph GT6   *Triumph Photo*

Standard-Triumph management never missed the chance to enter a product in international competition and Spitfires were raced and rallied extensively. The factory-sponsored teams of specially-built, much-modified fastbacks (pre-GT6) earned many trophies including first and second in class at Le Mans in 1965.

Originally dubbed "Spitfire 4", it became the Mark II in 1965 with minimal change. A 1296cc engine, much-improved top, exterior styling changes and a new interior created the Mark 3 in 1967, still with the original round-tailed body. A major change for 1971 launched the Mark IV with all-new bonnet assembly and squared-off rear styling with large, horizontal, tail-lights.

A further displacement change was made for 1973 and the 1500 Spitfire would be produced through 1980. The swing-axle rear suspension had been improved to eliminate handling problems and the car was a good performer. However, US Federal regulations eventually reduced power to an uncompetitive level in that primary market, and the car was purchased mainly on looks in its last couple of years.

There was no lack of power in the Triumph GT6, a fastback variation of the Spitfire produced from 1967 through 1973. Mounting a two-liter version of the Triumph six-cylinder engine, the little GT was as quick as the TR series and very smart looking as well. It used a Spitfire hood with a power bulge to cover the larger engine and its own rear styling. Once the swing-axles had been replaced by a sophisticated double-link rear suspension, the GT6 became a "mini E-Type" with only two disadvantages. It was hot inside and even people of medium height had little headroom.

The GT6 went through a Mark II stage, known as "GT6 Plus" in the United States, and became a Mark III with the same body modifications, front and rear, as the Spitfire, in 1971. Unfortunately, cost-cutting measures brought back the swing-axles in 1973 and the car was dropped after that model year.

A variation on the Herald, using Triumph's Vitesse name from the 1930s, was produced first with a 1596cc six-cylinder engine and later with the two-liter. Sedan and convertible were built but only the 1596cc convertible was sold briefly in the US as the Sports Six.

Spitfires and GT6s are also readily available to the US collector, at very reasonable prices. Parts supplies, with exceptions such as later GT6 Mk III bonnets, are excellent and the cars are still enjoyable to drive. Prices range from around $3000 for Spitfires up to near $10,000 for very good GT6s.

The last two cars to bear the TR prefix were the TR7 and TR8. They were the only Triumph sports cars conceived after the great merger of Leyland Motor Corporation (Triumph, Rover and Leyland Truck and Bus) and British Motor Holdings (Austin, MG, Morris, Jaguar, etc.) in 1968. Corporate considerations often took precedence at British Leyland and thus, the styling of the new Triumph TR7 was determined via competition between Triumph's designers and the group at Austin-Morris. The Austin-Morris effort won.

Triumph TR7   *Triumph Photo*

One of the very first aerodynamic wedge designs for a car, the TR7 styling was a "love it or hate it" matter from the first. The front was attractive but the short 85-inch wheelbase meant that it appeared fore-shortened from the side and the squared-off rear end was simply too high. An unfortunate curving style line on the side makes the rear seem even higher. Underneath, the car had the Triumph two-liter, all-aluminum four designed originally for use by SAAB, and a four-speed gearbox and rear axle assembly from the Austin Marina.

Production of the four-cylinder TR7 coupe began in 1974. The car was given a tremendous send-off to the press but poor performance, bad quality and the controversial styling meant it got very mixed reviews. The TR7 struggled until 1977 when the five-speed gearbox and much sturdier rear axle assembly from the Rover 3500 made a much-needed improvement. Later, production was moved from Liverpool to Triumph's factory in Coventry. Product quality improved dramatically; but it was too late, however, to make the car really popular despite the arrival of the convertible model.

The TR7 emerged first as a coupe due to anticipated US Federal regulations banning open cars. These regulations, which affected the planning of all of the world's car manufacturers, did not materialize and the partially engineered convertible project was brought on as quickly as possible. It was launched in 1978 and became a good seller because many of the objections to the styling were eliminated by the new top configuration. Special versions, such as the all-black spyder of 1980, were popular.

Despite being planned from the beginning, the TR8 was not introduced until 1980 and then only in North America. An abortive effort to build a 1978 model had begun at Liverpool, but only about 150 cars were built. The actual production TR8s, along with the 1980 and 1981 TR7s, were built at the Rover plant in Solihull.

The TR8 was not just a hot-rod TR7. Although dimensionally the same and looking identical to the four-cylinder car, the V8 TR was a slick, fast, solid vehicle. 125 mph top speed and acceleration 0-60 in the 8-second range put it in a class with many more famous cars. It was well-built and dependable, using the proven all-aluminum Rover 3.5-liter V8 and five-speed gearbox. Had it been available in the mid-1970s, in quantity, it might have helped put off the demise of Triumph. However, those "corporate considerations" including a shortage of the V8 engines, delayed the TR8 and it was built only in 1980 and 1981. A total of fewer than 3000 coupes and convertibles came off the line, all but 300 in 1980.

TR7 prices to collectors are low - close to Spitfire levels. The enthusiast who wants a car to drive may find a five-speed TR7 just the ticket. Low initial investment, excellent road handling and comfort and reasonable maintenance make the car a pleasure to drive, assuming the styling isn't a consideration. Large numbers were made with automatic and air conditioning. The cars are weather-tight and quiet. Pay attention to potential rust on wheel-arches and fender openings and watch for seepage around the head-gasket, indicating a possible warped cylinder head. Engine work is expensive and heads are difficult to find because so many were faulty. Electronic ignition modules are prone to failure and are expensive. The 1975-77 four-speed cars should be avoided due to poor performance and very bad quality.

Although the original 1978 pre-production cars, all of which were eventually sold in the United States, are not as desirable, all TR8s can be considered good investments for the collector. Priced between $9000 and $20,000, these potent cars avoid the flaws of the TR7 and rate very high for enjoyment. Items to watch on TR8 bodies are similar to the TR7.

Triumph's other collectible sports car of the 1970s was the Stag. One of a series of four-letter code-names such as Zest for TR4, Zobo for Herald and Bomb for Spitfire, the Stag designation was one that stuck. Larger than other sports models, the Stag shared platform and suspension components with the Triumph sedan, and was a four-seater with a removable hard top and permanent, Targa-style roll bar. It was trimmed in leather, sleek in appearance and priced to fit between the TR6 and the Jaguar E-Types.

Power for the Stag was a 3-liter V8 derived from the slant four. The Stag was available with a four-speed gearbox or automatic transmission, air conditioning and other luxury features. Announced in 1970, it was acclaimed for its appearance but proved disastrous in quality. It survived only three years, 1971-73, in the United States market and was available in England through 1977. The 1973 cars had most of the problems rectified, but the Triumph marketing organization in the US had no confidence in the car and dropped it.

The Stag is a classic sports tourer and a desirable collectors item. Engine parts, particularly cylinder heads and blocks, are very hard to find and electrical problems will be encountered, particularly in early cars. 1973 and later Stags suffer less from cooling system flaws, but at the cost of very high system pressure. Many Stags in the United States have had engine conversions to Ford or GM V6s because of failure of the original engines. Prices vary in the $10,000 - $20,000 range.

In the list of Triumph sedans of the sixties and seventies, the 2000-2.5 series deserves mention. The 2000, a Michelotti design powered by the six-cylinder engine was launched in 1963 and sold in the US from 1964 to 1967. In 2.5-liter and later 2500 guise, the car was produced until 1977 as a four-door and station wagon.

A later small sedan not imported into the US was the 1972-1980 Dolomite. A mid-size four-door sports sedan, the Dolomite had a 16-valve version of the TR7 four-cylinder engine which produced BMW 3-series performance and powered the car to many successes in European rallies in the 1970s. Some of the 16-valve engines were installed in TR7s sold in the UK and gave the car much better performance.

Triumph sports car production ceased in 1981. Triumph sedan production ended with the 1984 model year. However, the number of enthusiast cars built under the Triumph name guarantees the marque a secure future with collectors.

TRIUMPH CARS OF INTEREST TO COLLECTORS

Pre-War:
Super Seven, Gloria, Dolomite, Gloria Vitesse.

Post-War:

1800 roadster and sedan
Renown sedan
2000 roadster
Mayflower sedan
TR2, TR3, TR3A, TR3B roadsters
Italia coupe
TR4 and TR4A roadsters
TR5 and TR250 roadsters
TR6 roadster
TR7 and TR8 coupe and roadster
Stag convertible
2000 and 2.5 sedans
Herald and Vitesse sedan and convertible
Dolomite Sprint
Spitfire 4, Mk II, Mk III, Mk IV and 1500 roadsters
GT6 Mk 1, Mk II, GT6 Plus and Mk III

It should be noted that TR2 through TR6, Spitfire and Stag were all available with removable steel hardtops as original equipment.

HOW TO GET STARTED IN TRIUMPH

The best way to start is with membership in one of the Triumph clubs listed below. They'll help you find sources for parts and services.

Vintage Triumph Register
Box 36477
Grosse Pointe, MI   48236
201-691-8116
Founded 1974, 4,000 members, publishes newsletter and magazine.

Triumph Sports Six Club
3 Common Rise
Hitchin, Herts SG4 OHN
England
0462 56315
Founded 1977, 12,000 members, three publications

ABOUT THE AUTHOR

Mike Cook bought his first sports car in 1957, a Triumph TR2. Since then he has owned two TR3s, a TR4, a Spitfire, a GT6 and two TR6s, a 1975 example of which currently lives in his garage and refuses to leave. After college, Mike worked in his home town of Cincinnati for a few years, and moved to New York to become Assistant Advertising Manager for the Standard-Triumph Motor Car Company. When Triumph became part of British Leyland, Mike went along to become PR chief for the combined marques. While there, he wrote a book and many articles about Triumph and published a monthly newsletter for the Triumph Sports Car Association. He had a successful amateur racing career, always in Triumphs, competing a TR3, Spitfire, TR7 and TR8 at various times.

YEAR	LINE	Relative Condition: Worse ↔ Better		
		❸	❷	❶
1953—1955	TR2 Roadster	7000	10000	14000
1955—1957	TR3 Roadster	6500	9000	13000
1957—1962	TR3 A Roadster	6500	9000	13000
1962—1963	TR3 B Roadster	7000	9500	13500
1961—1964	TR4 Roadster	5000	7200	8500
1965—1968	TR4 A Roadster	5500	8000	10000
1963—1966	Spitfire Roadster	2500	4000	6000
1967—1973	Spitfire Roadster	2000	4000	5500
1966—1968	GT6 Mark I Coupe	1800	3500	5000
1969—1970	GT6+ Coupe	2000	3500	5500
1968	TR250 Roadster	6000	8000	10500
1969—1976	TR6 Roadster	4500	7500	11000
1970—1973	Stag Roadster	5500	8000	11000